Basic Bible Sermons on Easter

BASIC BIBLE SERMONS

ON

EASTER

Chevis F. Horne

BROADMAN PRESS
NASHVILLE, TENNESSEE

ISBN: 0-8054-2271-4
Dewey Decimal Classification: 252.63
Subject Heading: EASTER—SERMONS
Library of Congress Card Catalog Number: 89-29514

Printed in the United States of America

Unless otherwise stated, all Scripture quotations are from the *Revised Standard Version of the Bible,* copyrighted 1946, 1952, © 1971, 1973.

All Scriptures marked KJV are from the King James Version of the Bible.

Library of Congress Cataloging-in-Publication Data

Horne, Chevis F.
   Basic Bible sermons on Easter / Chevis F. Horne.
      p.   cm.
   ISBN 0-8054-2271-4 :
   1. Easter—Sermons.   2. Jesus Christ—Resurrection—Sermons.
3. Sermons, American.   4. Baptists—Sermons.   I. Title.
BV4259.H67   1990
252'.63—dc20   89-29514
                                                                    CIP

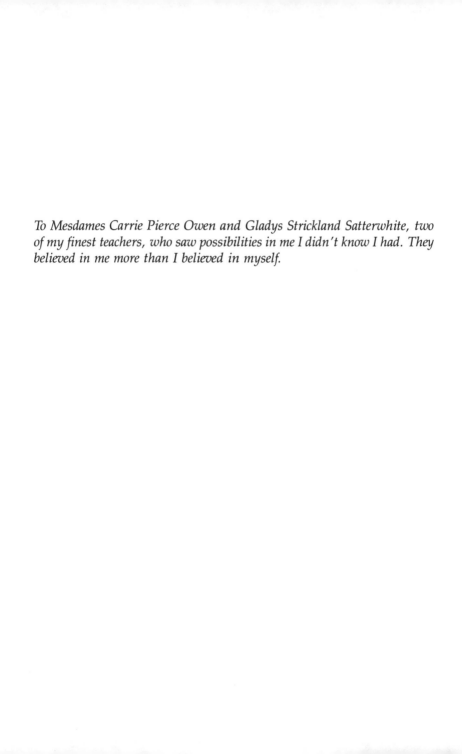

To Mesdames Carrie Pierce Owen and Gladys Strickland Satterwhite, two of my finest teachers, who saw possibilities in me I didn't know I had. They believed in me more than I believed in myself.

Contents

Foreword

What an honor to be asked to write a preliminary word for a book of sermons on one of the cardinal truths of our Christian faith by an outstanding preacher and a personal friend of more than fifty years!

The apostle Paul early recognized the significance of Jesus' resurrection in these words: "If Christ be not risen, then is our preaching vain, and your faith is also vain" (1 Cor. 15:14). Was not Paul saying that without the resurrection there is no gospel, no salvation, no hope, and no meaning? Without God's vindication of Jesus' obedience unto death on the cross, where is there any "good news"? Where is forgiveness? To what can we look forward? What does it all mean? What's the bottom line?

Without the resurrection, the cross is a tragedy and a most persuasive argument for atheism. Without the victory of God and His righteousness, we might as well leave our churches and "get all we can while the getting is good"—the pagan philosophy of the "me generation."

Thanks be to God! Jesus is risen from the dead: "the firstfruits of them that slept" (1 Cor. 15:20, KJV). That was the good news which stirred the ancient world, so the early church made Easter morn their holiest of days—centuries before Christmas was observed. It gave people faith to endure the persecutions, knowing that God would win in the end (Rev. 1:4-6). It brought forgiveness and acceptance; it gave hope and expectation; it supplied a motive for righteousness and meaning and purpose for living.

Early Baptists reacted against an over emphasis on special days, arguing that every day should honor our Lord's birth and resurrection. More recently, we have realized we can be so general that the particular truths can be dimmed and obscured, so Christmas and Easter now have prominent places in our worship. Alas, however, many preachers restrict messages on the resurrection to funeral mediations or to one sermon a year, and that one is shortened to allow time for an Easter cantata or special anthems by the choir.

In this volume the author, a choice proclaimer of "the unsearchable riches of Christ," corrects this imbalance and resets the resurrection as Christendom's most glorious gem of faith. He preaches anew that there is indeed "good news" for us and for our times.

The son of a Baptist minister and a devout mother, Chevis F. Horne is a graduate of Wake Forest University (A.B., 1936) and The Southern Baptist Theological Seminary (Th.M., 1939). Additional studies were done at Union Seminary in New York City, Yale University, and the School of Pastoral Care in Winston-Salem, North Carolina. He has been awarded two honorary doctorates from Wake Forest University and the University of Richmond.

After serving two years as an associate pastor in Martinsville, Virginia, Dr. Horne entered the Army as chaplain in 1942 and saw action in Europe. Upon discharge in 1945, he returned to Martinsville where he married Helen Ellett and resumed his associate pastorate at First Baptist Church. In 1947, Horne was made pastor and continued until retirement in 1979 when he was invited to Southeastern Baptist Seminary as visiting professor of preaching, a position he still holds.

In addition to his church and classroom duties, Horne has been active in his community and denomination, participating in civic clubs, family counseling, mental hygiene, human relations, interfaith conferences, and relief work. Horne's denominational activities include trusteeship at colleges and state agencies, lecturing at seminaries and on college campuses, presiding as moderator of associations, serving as chairperson of Christian Life Committees, leading the Baptist Pastors' Conference of his state, and presiding at the Baptist General Association of Virginia.

Prior to this volume, Horne published four books: *Crisis in the Pulpit* (1975), *Being Christian in Our Town* (1978), *Dynamic Preaching*

(1983), and *Preaching the Great Themes of the Bible* (1986). Horne continues to contribute articles to various religious journals and denominational publications.

He has traveled widely in Europe, the Near East, the Orient, and the South Pacific. In all of his ministry, Horne has been supported by Helen, his wife, who has shared in all that he has done.

Here is a deeply committed Christian with a highly educated and discerning mind, a warmhearted pastor with a sensitive social conscience, and a stimulating teacher with an evangelical concern.

Hear and heed this masterful preacher speak on a timely and eternal subject that is basic to our Christian faith, hope, and love: the resurrection.

James H. Blackmore,
Emeritus Professor
Southeastern Baptist Theological Seminary

Introduction

No empty tomb, no credible cross! No resurrection, no Christianity! These are radical statements, but true.

There are many decisive events in Christianity: the birth, life, and death of Jesus. But the resurrection of Jesus Christ is uniquely decisive.

These sermons are based mostly on great stories connected with Easter as found in our Gospels. That reminds us of something very important and very essential. Christianity is not a speculative system of thought. It is about real happenings, events, meetings, and encounters. These are best told by story, probably the most effective form of human communication. Someone says, "Once upon a time," and everybody listens. A story is about to be told. While the Bible has many literary forms, its basic one is story. Its other literary forms are set within the broad spectrum of story. The story is grounded in reality in a way other forms of communication are not. Life is story. Our Faith is story. Our Bible is story. Story was Jesus' favorite form of teaching and preaching. It should not be surprising that we are now talking about preaching as story.

The purpose of these sermons would be aborted if they became crutches, sparing us the task of sermon preparation with its reading, reflection, study, and, yes, even drudgery. I write them in the hope that they will help keep Easter faith alive in us, that the springs of this faith will remain fresh and flowing. One of the ironies of preaching is that often the springs of faith become sluggish, even when we are dealing with a great theme such as Easter. Our preaching is not scintillating. Our words seem lifeless—without power, falling like lead upon the ears of our hearers! Every preacher knows what I am talking about. A dry season of the soul may be upon us. We need to guard these springs. If *Basic Bible Sermons on Easter* could serve this purpose, even in a model way, I would be very happy.

Chevis F. Horne

1
Death and Resurrection

(1 Cor. 15:1-11)

When Paul looked at the heart of the Christian gospel, he saw an ellipse with the death and resurrection of Jesus as the foci. Therefore, he said in his first letter to the church at Corinth:

> I delivered to you as of first importance what I also received, that Christ died for our sins in accordance with the scriptures, that he was buried, that he was raised on the third day in accordance with the scriptures (1 Cor. 15:3-4).

I had been out of the seminary for several years before I understood what Paul meant. It was an illuminating experience. I knew Paul was saying that the gospel is the answer to the two great tragedies of human existence: sin and death. I realized that day that we have more than just good news. We have great news!

The Heart of the Gospel

In the death and resurrection of Jesus Christ, we come to the heart of our gospel: the answer to our sin and death.

Men and women the world over walk under the shadow of their guilt and into the night of their death. We are sinners. We set our little wills against the will of God. We are rebels, estranged from God and cut off from Him. We are separated from our brothers and sisters.

All of us die. All things we create will eventually perish. We build our mortality into everything we make.

When we were building our church sanctuary, the architect said to me one day: "Let me tell you a little about my philosophy of architecture and symbolism. I think both should express some basic tenet of the Christian faith. They must serve some theological purpose. Do you have any ideas?"

I did have some ideas. I talked with him about Paul's concept of how Christ, in His death and resurrection, answered the problems of our sin and death. Let our architecture and symbolism become the media of this good news.

He assured me it would be easy. "We can suspend a cross," he said, "from the chancel ceiling and then transcend the cross with a resurrection window." This he did with powerful effect on our worshipers.

I remember the day some school children came to study our architecture and symbolism. I knew I had a hard task. How could I get and hold their attention. I began, only to discover that their eyes were moving everywhere, and I was sure that their minds were equally as restless. Then I pointed to the cross and said: "That cross in the time of Jesus was what the electric chair is in our own day. It was an instrument of death, and Jesus was put to death on a cross. He died for you and me and the whole world." Now, the children were listening.

Then we moved to the resurrection window, and I pointed to Jesus who was emerging from the tomb, His left leg having cleared it. "You will notice," I observed, "that in His left hand He carries a banner of victory over death. This tells us that He has conquered death. His right hand is raised in blessing. That is the way He tells us that He loves and cares for us."

I continued: "The meaning of the cross and resurrection window is that Jesus Christ—the strong One who lived, died for us, and now lives forevermore—loves and cares for us. And since He does, He can forgive our sins and give us life." The children were now caught up in rapt attention. But why? It did not take long to find the answer. I was saying what the human heart wants to hear above all things else. It cries out for forgiveness and for life. It is the deepest cry of all. The gospel of Jesus Christ can answer that cry.[1]

The Answer to Our Sins

The cross is the answer to our sins for several reasons.

First Christ died on the cross for me and for the entire world. He got beneath the terrible weight of my guilt and bore it far away.

Paul tells us, "God shows his love for us in that while we were yet sinners Christ died for us" (Rom. 5:8). He didn't wait until we were older, wiser, reformed, or better. He died for us while we were yet sinners.

There is Jesus on His cross. Into His peace goes my anxiety, into His strength my weakness, into His love my bitterness, into His purity my impurity, and into His sinlessness my sin. He bears them all that He may turn and speak a free forgiveness.

Paul could speak of Christ as the One "who loved me and gave himself for me" (Gal. 2:20). I must feel that way about Christ. I can never sense the wonder of Christ's death unless I take it personally. I am sure that God knows the name of all things He has created, but I want Him to know my name. I know that there is enough grace in Jesus Christ to cover the sins of the entire world, but I want to know that He has forgiven me. I know that Christ died for this estranged world, but I want to know that He died for me.

We visited the Passion Play in Oberammergau, Germany, in 1980. There we saw the powerful drama that depicts Jesus' last week on earth, including His resurrection. As we were leaving that Bavarian town, the oldest person in our group, a woman who was eighty-three said, "The death of Jesus means so much to me." Then with strong emotion she continued, "But the thing that means most to me is that He died for me." That is the way Paul felt, and that is the way I should feel.

Wherever Christianity goes it is known by the cross, its basic symbol. Yet if Jesus had died some other way, the instrument of His death, no matter what, would have been the symbol identifying His religion. If He had been stoned, the symbol of our religion would be a stone; if hanged, a hangman's noose.

Further, the cross is where we are judged.

The cross of Jesus exposes and judges sin more ruthlessly than anywhere else. Yet it is not so much the crass, vulgar, and profane sins exposed there as the subtle, respectable, and socially acceptable ones. Theft, robbery, prostitution, and murder do not need to be exposed; they expose themselves. Sins that wear cloaks of respectability, more than any other kind, are disrobed and left in their stark nakedness at the cross of Jesus.

Jesus was not put to death by the underworld. No, the most respectable forces of the ancient world put Jesus to death. Religion, the custodian of faith and morality, and the state, the dispenser of justice and the keeper of the social order, joined hands to put Him to death. At the cross of Jesus we see not how bad bad men are, but how bad "good" men are.

If a hoodlum had stabbed Jesus to death in a back alley, people would have called it murder. But since respectable forces put Him to death by due process of law, they called it justice. In the sight of God, however, and now in the eyes of history, the hearts of Caiphas and Pilate as well as His other accusers were just as murderous as would have been the heart of a hoodlum who might have stabbed Him to death.

Finally, if the cross of Jesus is where Christ died for me and where I am judged: it is also the place where I am forgiven. There, the grace of God is poured out for the forgiveness of sins as nowhere else. There, I learn I am forgiven in grace, that salvation is a gift.

I bring empty hands to Christ and say to Him, "I wish I had something good to bring You, but I don't." Then He looks at my poor empty hands and says a most wonderful thing: "If you had all the moral wealth in the universe, You could not buy My salvation. It is of grace, it is a gift. Your empty hands are enough."

One of my best friends was an arrested alcoholic. I saw him "hit bottom" and go away to a hospital to be "dried out." A little nurse there was one of the most caring and compassionate people the man had known. She told him one day that a representative of Alcoholics Anonymous would speak that night at 7:30, and she urged him to attend. My friend said he had a poker game scheduled, but he could not refuse the invitation of one who had been so kind to him. So at 7:30, the man was a part of the group gathered to hear the speaker, a young man in his middle thirties. He had rapidly climbed the ladder of success and because of alcoholism had fallen just as precipitously. The young man told his story. He was now on the way back to wholeness and success. As he neared the end of his talk, he said, "Is there one of you fellows who would like to be sober again?" My friend said his hand shot up; he could not hold it down. He exclaimed: "Sir, I would give every cent I've got to sober again." The speaker responded, "My friend, you can be sober again, and it won't cost you a penny." So Christ from His cross says to me, "You can be saved, and it won't cost you a penny. My salvation is a gift."

The Answer to Our Death

If the cross is the answer to our sin, then the resurrection of Jesus is the answer to our death.

Easter is about Christ meeting death head-on in its own territory—a tomb—and He won. He conquered death and offers life, as He does forgiveness, as a gift.

There are many bondages from which men and women have had hope for escape. But death is one bondage from which there has been no hope. There are prisons, many from which we can go free, but there is one prison from which we can never go free by our own efforts: the prison of death. Our feeble hands cannot tear away the bars. Frantically, we beat our heads upon those bars, but to no avail. Only one Person has been able to enter that prison and lift the bars away—Jesus Christ, and He did it on Easter.

Easter morning is different from all other mornings. It flooded our world with a strange new light, and all the darkness of the universe cannot put it out. It is light that has imperishable life.

I heard Joseph R. Sizoo preach in 1941 in a church in New York City. It was an evening service, and not many people were present. The church was depressed as it was about to be swallowed up by a vast secular city. Yet Sizoo spoke with hope that night. It was as if he had an easel in the pulpit with him. He was an artist painting a dawn, and what a dawn it was! As he came near the end of the sermon, he said: "Once the dawn has started, nothing can stop it." That was almost fifty years ago, and it is as fresh in my memory today as when I first heard it. During the years in times of discouragement and depression I have heard the voice of Sizoo saying: "Once the dawn has started, nothing can stop it."

Easter was a burst of light, a dawn, a daybreak, and nothing can ever put out its light.

It is little wonder you find an invincibility in the New Testament. It says such radical and exciting things: "O death, where is thy victory? O death, where is thy sting?" (1 Cor. 15:55). "No, in all these things we are more than conquerors through him who loved us" (Rom. 8:37). "The darkness is passing away and the true light is already shining" (1 John 2:8). "The kingdom of the world has become the kingdom of our Lord and of his Christ, and he shall reign for ever and ever" (Rev. 11:15). All these bold declarations were made after Easter.

Easter has changed the human landscape, bringing hope, life, and light into the shadows. The new order of life has been thrust into the old order of death.

It should be said that the cross and the resurrection must be held together. Historically, they are only three days apart, but in terms of faith they are much closer. It is as if they are two sides of the same event. They are like the palm and back of my hand which cannot be separated without destroying my hand. Without the resurrection of Jesus, His death would be sheer tragedy. Without His death, we cannot be sure that the resurrection is anything more than brute power. But holding them together, we can be sure that we meet the same kind of power in both—the mighty love of God. We can trust that love.

Note

1. Chevis F. Horne, *Preaching the Great Themes of the Bible* (Nashville: Broadman Press, 1986), 92-93.

2
The Easter Story

(Mark 16:1-8)

One of the best-known stories of the Christian faith is that of Easter. People indicate this by their response. Our churches are more crowded on Easter than any other day. Throngs of people will attend churches throughout the world. They come again, not to hear a new story but an old one—the Easter story.

They come to feel Easter's accent on life, to listen to the startling announcement: "He has risen, he is not here; and to hear these thunderous words: "Death is swallowed up in victory" (1 Cor. 15:54).

People come to see through the shadows and darkness of mortal life some light that will never go out, to hear beyond the sad, sweet music of our mortality the strain of some eternal theme.

Those in darkness seek a path to light. Easter leads us that way, to the other side of darkness where the light of morning will not fail.

About a Man

Easter is a story about a man who lived, died, and left behind Him an empty tomb.

He was a strange man, this Christ of Easter. There was a light in His eyes that exposed the shadows in the eyes of other persons, a goodness that uncovered the evil in human hearts, a gentleness that exposed human ruthlessness, and a love that made obvious, by contrast, human bitterness and hatred of the human heart.

Love was the overarching quality of Jesus' life. He loved nature with its green fields, dawns and sunsets, bright days and starry nights. He loved friends, the demands of honest work, and the privilege of service. He loved life and found it painful to give up. He loved more the doing of his Father's will with its risks and high adventure than His own security. He loved the life of the world more than His own life.

There is a Gaelic legend that tells about an eagle swooping down and carrying a little baby to its lofty aerie. The strong men of the village tried to scale the high and rugged cliff, but each in turn failed. Then past them went a frail woman. Up, up she climbed to the sheer precipice and after a long time she returned, bringing the baby in a shawl. How did she do it, the strong men asked in amazement? Then she told the secret of her almost inhuman strength: "I am the baby's mother." Her love enabled her, frail as she was, to outdistance the strong men of the village.

The wonderful love of Jesus, like the love of that woman, allowed Him to outdistance others. Yet, this worked against Him. He exposed their slow, plodding, and devious ways, their cowardice in the face of hard demands, and their desire to save their own lives rather than the life of the ancient world. But men do not like to be outdistanced, have their weaknesses revealed, and their security threatened, so they put Him to death. He died on Good Friday the death of a criminal among criminals. His death was the most shameful kind of the world, but it was the one saving death of all history. He was buried in a tomb not far from where He died.

The tomb could not hold Him. Early on the first day of the week some women went to the sepulcher to anoint His body with spices. There they heard an announcement that shocked them and continues to startle the world: "He has risen, he is not here" Mark 16:6.

He was dead but He has risen. That is the good news of Easter.

A man, passing along a street, saw a boy studying a picture of the crucifixion in a store window and stopped to talk with him. The lad indicated how earnest he was: "That man on the cross is Jesus," the boy said, "and the woman crying is His mother. And the Roman soldier put Him to death."

The man moved on to hear hurrying feet behind him. It was the boy, who continued: "And mister, I forgot to tell you—He rose again."

So every Easter comes with the glad exclamation, "He is risen!"
A lovely woman used to greet me on Easter morning: "Christ is risen today." And knowing she was using an Easter greeting from Old Russia, I would respond: "He is risen indeed."

About Power

Easter is a story about power.

As the women made their way to the tomb, they kept asking themselves a troubling question: "Who will roll away the stone for us from the door of the tomb?" (Mark 16:3).

A huge stone blocked the doorway to the sepulcher. It was big and heavy, beyond the strength of the women. Yet when they arrived, they discovered that they had worried needlessly. The stone had been rolled way. More than that, the power of death had been shattered. Jesus Christ had broken free of death and was the living, reigning Lord of life. Obviously, power had been at work on Easter morning.

The early Christians lived in the awareness of that power. Weak as they were, it turned them into invincible persons.

Paul gave away the secret of his victorious life: "that I may know him and the power of his resurrection" (Phil. 3:10).

The mighty strength of Easter turned the funeral dirge into a shout of victory: "O death, where is thy sting? O grave, where is thy victory?" (1 Cor. 15:55, KJV) Only power can do that.

Christians down the centuries, often knocked to their knees by the hard blows of life, have felt this wonderful power. It was as if they were being carried on the mighty tides of Easter that shout at every turn of the bend: "Christ is risen!"

Harold E. Luccock told about a man looking over the Grand Canyon for the first time and exclaiming: "Something must have happened there." Power carved the canyon, tremendous power. Men and women have had something of that feeling as they have looked back on the empty tomb through the light of Easter morning.

About Victory

If Easter is a story about power, it is also a story about victory. It is about victory we can never win.

The Bible tells us that death is our last and most powerful enemy. We engage this terrible monster over and over again along the journey of life, and we win some skirmishes. Medical science is helping us to win more of these, but not even medical science in its wildest dreams believes that we can conquer this enemy. We all have a final engagement with death, and there is no question who will win. But Jesus Christ has met death where death is king—in a tomb, and He has won the victory we always lose.

The story is about a man who went into a tomb and tore its bars away. So death has looked different since that first Easter. In some real sense, its power has been shattered. Because Easter is about victory, we can live, even die, with a strong sense of confidence.

Dr. Elizabeth Kübler-Ross, a psychiatrist who spent her professional life working with terminally ill people, tells about children dying. She has never known a terminally ill child who didn't believe in life beyond death. The children will create symbols that point to the future life. They seem to have an intuitive grasp of a dimension of reality that adults often lose.

Kübler-Ross tells about a little boy who, along with his mother had accepted the reality of his impending death. He and his mother had worked through the fear of his death, so they could talk naturally about it. The little boy had earlier lost a friend whose name was Beth Ann. One day his mother, speaking of his approaching death, asked: "And what do you want?" "As we go to the cemetery," he said, "Turn on the lights in the ambulance, and turn the siren on loud, so Beth Ann will know I am coming." No defeat there. Only victory!

About Hope

Easter is a story of hope. It enables us to stand on the brink of death, look across its dark chasm, and by faith see the hills of life where day is always breaking. It gives hope without which we cannot live.

Kübler-Ross also tells about an attendant she worked with who had a strange calming effect on highly agitated patients. This woman grew up in poverty and knew what it was to be hungry. Kübler-Ross had often seen her come to the bedside of a patient who was extremely anxious and apprehensive, speak a few words, and leave the patient calm and composed. Kübler-Ross couldn't do that. What secret did this simple woman have that she, the professional doctor, did not know? One day she asked the attendant: "What do you say to these disturbed patients that leaves them so calm?" The reply was, "I say the simplest thing to them. I tell them it's not so bad."[1]

That is what the early Christians essentially said about death: it's not so bad. They took their vocabulary list and marked out the word *death*. They no longer spoke of their loved ones as being dead but as being asleep in Jesus. Paul could say to those early Christians who felt the pain of separation from those they had lost by death: "But we would not have you ignorant, brethren, concerning those who are asleep, that you may not grieve as others do who have no hope" (1 Thess. 4:13).

Edward Wilson was with Captain Scott at the south pole. Wilson wrote Scott's wife: "If this letter reaches you, Bill and I will have gone together. We are very near it now and should like you to know how splendid he was at the end. His eyes have a comfortable blue look of hope, and his mind is peaceful with the satisfaction of his faith, in regarding himself as a part of the scheme of the Almighty."

Easter allows a person to die that way—in hope.

About Our Story

We face the danger allowing Easter to be a story far in the past. We will never know its wonder unless it enters the present moment. We must let the story of Easter become our story. How can this be?

We have to know that the Easter story is about our death. It is about my death, the death of my wife, and the death of my child. Easter is about the death of each of us.

Further, we have to realize that Jesus Christ won the victory over death, not for Himself alone but for all of us. Dietrich Bonhoeffer spoke of Jesus as the "man for others." There was nothing selfish in Him. Whatever He did, He did for others. He lived for others, He died for others, and He was resurrected for others. I can say: "Jesus Christ won for me."

Also, we have to accept the Christ of Easter. We have to trust Him, surrender to Him, and confess Him as Savior and Lord. We say with Thomas, "My Lord and my God!" (John 20:28).

Finally, we have to know that the resurrected Christ is more than a remote figure of the past. He is the living, reigning Lord of life and history, set free from Roman sword and spear, and all the forces that shackle us. He is with us.

Paul had in mind the living Christ when he wrote: "For you have died, and your life is hid with Christ in God" (Col. 3:3). We experience this when the Easter story becomes our own. We find a hiding place in Him that is beyond the destructive reach of tragedy.

I remember my ministry many years ago to a dear friend dying of cancer. One day when I was going to the hospital to see her, I met one of her friends who sent a message of great comfort and hope. "Tell Sue," she said, "that her life is hid with Christ in God. There, nothing can hurt her."

The plea is that we will allow the Easter story to pass over into personal history, that it may become our story. In so doing let us walk out into the beauty of this Easter Day with undaunted hope and courage.

Note

1. Chevis F. Horne, *Preaching the Great Themes of the Bible* (Nashville: Broadman Press, 1986), 100.

3
Daybreak Over an Empty Tomb

(Matt. 28:1-10)

The Easter story has daybreak as its setting. Matthew sets his story "toward the dawn of the first day of the week;" Mark, "very early . . . when the sun had risen;" and Luke, "at early dawn." Since that day, streaks of light in the east on Easter morning call for worship to begin. We hold Easter sunrise services because the Easter story has dawn for its setting.

There was something different about that first Easter morning. Before, mornings had broken in a world where tombs held their victims. But that morning, daybreak was over an empty tomb. A tomb had been forced to give up its victim who had become Conqueror of death. He broke the bonds of death, snapped its chains, and freed Himself of life's ultimate imprisonment.

Use of Light

Light conveys beautiful, meaningful imagery. We speak of dawns and sunsets, starry nights, and shafts of light in the darkness. What could be lovelier? The Easter story is in keeping with the Bible's extensive use of light.

The Bible begins and ends with light. The first thing God created was light. God looked out upon a vast darkness and said, "Let there be light" (Gen. 1:3). And there was light. God created light before He did luminary-producing bodies. This order has a theological significance.

The Bible ends with a city, the new Jerusalem, that is perfectly lighted. There is not a shadow or trace of darkness in it. "And the city has no need of sun or moon to shine upon it," we are told, "for the glory of God is its light, and its lamp is the Lamb. . . . and its gates shall never be shut by day—and there shall be no night there" (Rev. 21:23,25).

When the Bible speaks of light it usually means more than luminous physical energy. Light is normally used in a metaphorical sense. It represents something greater than itself. The Bible knows of dawns and mornings that are reaching beyond themselves.

Light represents the presence and glory of God, the nature of God, the truth of God, and the disclosure of God. Light is even used to personalize God. When the Bible speaks of the light of God's face, it represents Him as being personal, "Lift up the light of thy countenance upon us, O Lord!" implored the psalmist (Ps. 4:6).

Who can forget that lovely benediction which occurs where you would hardly expect it, in a book concerned with a census which is so dull and prosaic? It speaks of God as being personal, something the human heart craves to hear:

> The Lord bless you, and keep you:
> The Lord make his face to shine upon you, and be gracious to you:
> The Lord lift up his countenance upon you, and give you peace
> (Num. 6:24-25).

Light may mean the Word of God. "Thy word is a lamp to my feet," exclaimed the psalmist, "and a light to my path" (Ps. 119:105).

The New Testament makes three brave attempts to define God: "God is spirit," "God is love," and "God is light." They are so simple and yet so profound.

Love is the word that best describes God, but next is the word *light*. "God is light," declares John, "and in him is no darkness at all" (1 John 1:5).

Light is associated with Jesus. His birth is spoken of as a "dayspring from on high" (Luke 1:78, KJV). The birth of Jesus was announced to shepherds while they tended their sheep by night, and "the glory of the Lord shone round about them" (Luke 2:9, KJV). The wise men followed a brilliant star "til it came to rest over the place where the child was" (Matt. 2:9). John, in the prologue to his Gospel, says: "In him was life, and the life was the light of men"

(John 1:4). And Jesus said about himself: "I am the light of the world" (John 9:5).

It would be strange indeed if the Gospels, when telling about the resurrection of Jesus, did not employ the use of light. This they did. The Synoptic Gospels set their stories at dawn, just when the sun was making ready to flood the world with light, driving away the darkness. The angel who announced to the women at the tomb that Jesus was risen is described as one whose "appearance was like lightning, and his raiment white as snow."

Once more light is pointing beyond itself. It is more than luminous physical energy overflowing the world. It has theological meaning. It is a morning telling of a new day, with a new victory, new hope, and new life. It is daybreak over an empty tomb telling of a victory over death.

What Is the Daybreak Saying?

But more specifically, what is this daybreak saying? What is it announcing? Let me suggest four things.

First, Jesus Christ is alive.

Some women who loved Jesus had come to anoint His body. It was the last loving thing they could do for Him, they thought. But what a surprise they got! An angel, clothed in light, said to them: "Do not be afraid; for I know that you seek Jesus who was crucified. He is not here; for he has risen, as he said" (Matt. 28:5-6). And by the faint light of the early dawn, they looked into Jesus' tomb and saw that it was empty.

The great exclamation of Easter is: Christ is risen!

I have mentioned Easter sunrise services. One of the best known is the Moravian service held at Old Salem, Winston-Salem, North Carolina. The Moravian sunrise service has had a continuous history for over 200 years, having originated in Herrnhut, Saxony, a village established by some religious refugees on the estate of Count Nikolaus von Zinzendorf, the founder of Moravian Church. On Easter Sunday in 1732, before dawn, a group of earnest young men met on "God's acre," which was a cemetery, to sing hymns and meditate on the meaning of Christ's death and resurrection. As they stood amid the simply marked graves, singing their hymns of hope and victory, and watching the rising sun drive darkness from the hills and valleys, they experienced in a new way and a new depth the meaning of the resurrection. And thus began the meaningful Moravian Easter sunrise service with its long and unbroken history.

About two o'clock on Easter morning, the Easter band assembles and disperses in groups throughout Old Salem, playing Easter chorales, partly to remind all listeners of the resurrection and partly to awaken people for the sunrise service to follow. The first chorale played by each group is: "Sleepers, wake!"

A vast congregation assembles outside the Home Moravian Church before dawn. With the first signs of day in the east, the minister exclaims: "The Lord is risen!" The people respond, "The Lord is risen indeed!" Then the choir and congregation sing triumphantly:

> Hail, all hail, victorious Lord and Saviour,
> Thou hast burst the bonds of death.

Thus the tone of the service, one of triumph, hope, and affirmation, is set.

Having completed the first part of the service at the church, the great throne of worshipers, assisted by 400 ushers, moves to God's Acre. A band of 500 members, divided into six groups, plays Moravian chorales antiphonally as the worshipers move to the cemetery. There among the graves, marked by simple recumbent stones which remind them of the democracy of death, they continue their affirmation and worship of their risen Lord. The great band merges and continues to play their triumphant Moravian chorales. The worship is concluded in a cemetery like the one where the First Easter occurred.

So in many places, millions of people declare in moving and dramatic ways just at the rising of the sun that Jesus Christ is risen. And all through Easter Sunday, people continue their worship of Christ who was dead but is alive forevermore.

Second, the cross of Jesus was victorious.

The cross of Jesus on the day of His death looked like shameful defeat. It seemed that He who had offered such hope to His people had failed them miserably. The light that shone so brightly flickered so low. Jesus had gotten caught in the dark winds of fear, prejudice, injustice, and sin, and those winds seemed to have blown out the light that was in Him. The darkness in His enemies seemed to be so much stronger than the light that was in Him.

Even nature responded to the darkness of that hour. Matthew tells us that "from the sixth hour there was darkness over all the land until the ninth hour" (27:45). Thus, from noon to three o'clock the land lay under a blanket of heavy darkness.

But Easter changed all of that. The light that was in Jesus had not really gone out while Jesus was on the cross, and Easter fanned that light into glory and power. The cross of Jesus, like His resurrection, was God's mighty act for our salvation.

A copy of *Good News for Modern Man* fell into the hands of a prisoner in Australia. At the beginning of the sixth chapter of Romans, there is an illustration captioned: "Set Free from the Power of Sin." A man burdened with a heavy load of guilt approaches the cross of Jesus and drops his intolerable burden at the foot of the cross. He moves beyond the cross free of his terrible burden. The prisoner, looking at the sketch, said: "I am that man." And he did what that man had done. He dropped his crushing load of sin and shame at the foot of Jesus' cross, and he experienced Christ's wonderful release, freedom, forgiveness, and new life.

Third, the power of death has been broken.

When dawn broke the previous day, Jesus' tomb looked so invincible. Pilate had done his best to secure it. Matthew tells us: "Pilate said to them, 'You have a guard of soldiers; go, make it as secure as you can.' So they went and made the sepulchre secure by sealing the stone and setting a guard" (27:65-66).

It looked so impregnable. Death always looks that way. Who has not felt what seems to be the terrible finality of death? But that tomb was not impregnable, and death is not invincible.

I remember Anzio Beach from World War II. In our briefing just after sailing from Naples, we were told the ships that carried us to Anzio would leave immediately for other parts. We would not have the backing of any kind of sea power. If we could not hold our ground and push our enemies back, they would drive us into the sea. I remember how our soldiers fought and how they died. Many of them had young wives and small children back in the states. Others had sweethearts waiting for them, and they dreamed of love, marriage, and children. I used to go to the cemetery there and see the long rows of white crosses interspersed with stars of David. Among the fallen was a young man I had known and been very fond of fourteen or fifteen years earlier. For two years I had driven a school bus and carried him to and from school. He was so alive and so full of himself in a wholesome sort of way. I had seen him once again for only a few minutes just before we sailed for Anzio. Somewhere in that cemetery was Paul. A great heaviness and gloom hung over the place. A thousand ordinary mornings, no matter how glorious, could never lift the gloom from this or any other cemetery. Only one morning can do that. That is Easter morning announcing that the power of death has been broken.

Fourth, life is fulfilled beyond the grave.

He who came forth from the tomb on Easter morning will not leave us there. He has said: "Because I live, you shall also live." He will see to it that our lives are fulfilled beyond the grave.

Several years ago I visited a historic cemetery in eastern Virginia. I was impressed by the large number of children as well as young women buried there, some of them in their thirties, many of whom had died in childbirth. *Must this be the end of those who were so young?* I asked.

What about babies that die? Pallbearers aren't needed. The undertaker takes the little casket in his arms. The baby didn't know what it was to love, laugh, play, or have friends; never knew the thrill of taking a first step or saying a first word; never felt the cool earth beneath bare feet nor the puff of fresh air in the face during a hot day; never knew the joy of learning, nor sensed the wonder of life. Must life end before it begins?

William Barclay in his autobiography pondered the mystery of those who die so young. "In this world young lives are cut off too soon" he wrote, "and often in a way that just does not make sense.

If there is no place in which lives receive their chance to flourish, to blossom in their beauty, to realize their potential, to be what this life never allowed them to be, then it is not love which is at the center of the world."

What about young people who die while standing on the threshold of success and achievement where hope is being fulfilled? Or young adults struck down in the midst of their best years when they are needed and loved so much?

Even old people die with hopes unfulfilled and a sense of life being unfinished. Victor Hugo, when an old man, wrote:

> For half a century I have been outpouring my volumes of thought in prose and verse, in history, in philosophy, drama, romance, ode, and ballad, yet, I appear to myself not to have said a thousandth part of what is within me; and when I am laid in the tomb I shall not reckon that my life is finished.[1]

No matter how old or how young, we die with an unfinished agenda. The question is: Is there a place and time when the agenda can be finished? Easter says there is.

I sometimes think of the great moments of my life. They have often happened in unlikely places and unexpected times. I remember standing at the head of the grave of a friend, ready to give the committal service. I realized he was being buried facing the east, not the west; the sunrise, not the sunset; the morning not the night. It was as if we believed he was not through with life. Later, his family placed a marker at the grave, cutting verses of faith upon it, and carving symbols of hope. You can do that it you believe life is fulfilled in dimensions beyond the grave. The daybreak over an empty tomb says it is.

What a wonderful day this is! Our risen Lord is free of all things that would bind Him. In great love and power, He wants to set us free and give us life. While we stand in the light of Easter morning, He calls us to love, trust, and follow Him.

Note

1. Alfred Barbour, trans. by Ellen F. Brewer, *Victor Hugo and His Time* (Harper and Bros., 1882), 254.

4
That First Easter Night

(John 20:19-25)

That first Easter night found the disciples behind locked doors. John introduces his narrative of that evening like this: "On the evening of that day, the first day of the week, the doors being shut where the disciples were, for fear of the Jews, Jesus came and stood among them and said to them, 'Peace be with you.'"

Their fear was stronger than chains, shackles, and prison bars. It was more powerful than the locks on those doors. Their hearts had become fortresses that held them prisoners of fear. Into that situation Jesus came, and His presence made all the difference in the world.

Among Them

Jesus did not hold Himself aloof from the pain and fear of His disciples. He came and stood in their midst. He cared about them. He had promised to come back to them, and He did.

The reality of evil and suffering puzzles the human mind more than all else. The questions they provoke are so tantalizing, so unanswerable. Why? Why? Why? we ask. Often we do not get an answer. But we get something better—the assurance that Christ is with us, that He has not held Himself apart from our pain and tragedy. He got caught in the cross fires of our greed and anger, the blows that bludgeon us fell on Him, and He has braved those powerful currents that sweep us far out to sea. God has shared our tragedy, too.

There is an old Italian painting that pictures Jesus on His cross. Behind Him, in the shadows, is God His Father. The spikes that are driven into His hands never stop until they have pierced the hands of God. Jesus suffers, and God suffers.

We have no surer sign of God being among us than the incarnation. God clothed Himself in our frail and fragile form and came among us. "The Word became flesh," John tells us, "and dwelt among us, full of grace and truth" (John 1:14). God was not willing to dwell above us or far away from us. He knew how lonely, alienated, broken, and sinful we are. He could save us best, not at a distance, but by being with us.

Incarnation has so much to tell us about who pastors should be and what preaching at its best is. Pastors are to be with their people. They cannot be aloof from their people during the week and effective in the pulpit on Sunday morning. A pastor must enter those prisons, be they real or psychological, that hold people in bondage. The pastor must be with the people, must share their hopes and fears, laugh with them, and weep with them.

Peace

When Jesus came among His disciples, He gave them a familiar greeting: "Peace be with you." This was a common greeting, like our *good morning,* yet with a richer and deeper meaning. The Hebrew word for peace is *shalom.* It is one of the most meaningful words in the Hebrew vocabulary. It means much more than the absence of conflict and tension. It conveys the idea of total well-being. So as the disciples greeted each other in that manner in the early morning; they were saying, "May you be at peace today with those with whom you work; may you be at peace with your family, friends, and neighbors; may you be at peace with yourself; and may you be at peace with God."

Three artists were asked to represent the idea of peace. One painted a dreamy landscape. It was as if nature were falling asleep. The second one painted a lake that was very peaceful at sundown. There wasn't a ripple on its surface. The third artist painted a mountain being rent by a powerful storm. Trees were being uprooted and large boulders were being tumbled down the side of the mountain. But nestled in the cleft of a rock was a little bird, unafraid, enjoying perfect peace. That little bird was experiencing *shalom*.

The Gospel writers found the existing literary forms inadequate to express their faith in Jesus. Those forms did not have the flexibility and resilience to tell their story. They had new wine, and the existent literary forms were like old wineskins. They therefore created a new literary form—the Gospel—through which to express their faith in Jesus.

But Paul, in writing his letters, used the contemporary letter form. He put new truth in old forms.

Letters typically began with a greeting. The writer usually simply said, "greeting." Paul had something much better. His greeting became: "Grace to you and peace from God our Father and the Lord Jesus Christ" (Rom. 1:7). This he used in all his letters, and in so doing gave the reality of peace a heightened meaning. He did this by coupling the idea of grace with it. It was grace and peace. Grace always came first. Paul knew he could not have peace in its deeper dimension without grace. Therefore peace was something one received, more a gift than an achievement.

Grace was God's love that we could never earn or deserve. It was God's unmerited favor. God took the initiative. He didn't wait until we were better. He loved us while we were His enemies, hostile and alienated. That is God's grace. There is no way of experiencing peace on its deepest levels without it.

Never in the history of the world has peace been needed so much as now, and never has peacemaking been so urgent. Our hour is different from all others. Never before have we held such awesome power—which can destroy all life on our planet—in our hands. The shadow of a nuclear war lies across the landscape of our modern world. It matters not what our agendas are, peacemaking should head them all. We should be saying to our world, "Peace be unto you." We should be doing those things that make for peace.

Marks of Identification

When Jesus greeted His disciples, He "showed them his hands and his side" (v. 20). The prints of the Roman nails were still in His hands, and the wounds made by the sword were still in His side.

These marks identified Him as the One who had been put to death three days earlier. The One who had died and the One who had been resurrected were the same person.

But there is an even deeper identification. He is the One who through suffering love saves and redeems us. Salvation is never cheap. It is costly to redeem people. The pierced hands and wounded side tell how costly it is.

When Faithful in *Pilgrim's Progress* was being mercilessly treated by someone who was overpowering him, "one came by, and bid him forbear, I did not know him at first; but as he went by, I perceived the holes in his hands and his side; then I concluded that he was our Lord."[1]

Sacrifice seems to be built into the very structure of life. Life is constantly issuing from death. Jesus said a grain of wheat cannot release the life that is within it unless it falls into the ground and dies. The only way a stream can save itself is to give itself away. The only living streams are flowing ones. When a stream refuses to give itself away, it stagnates and becomes a breeding place of disease and death. Jesus said the only way a person can save life is to give it away.

Jesus did not evade the basic law of sacrifice. He submitted to it. He fulfilled Isaiah's vision of the Suffering Servant who "was wounded for our transgressions, he was bruised for our iniquities" (Isa. 53:5, KJV). "With his stripes we are healed."

John's Pentecost

After greeting them the second time Jesus said to His disciples: "As the Father has sent me, even so I send you." Having said this to them, He breathed on them and said, "Receive the Holy Spirit" (v. 21). This has been called John's pentecost.

In biblical thought, breath and wind can suggest the reality of spirit. The Hebrew *ruah* and the Greek *pneuma* can be translated breath or wind. Spirit, like breath and wind, is unseen and intangible. Yet you can feel its vitality and power just as you can that of breath and wind. Therefore Jesus breathed on His disciples as He gave them the Spirit of God.

John may have had in mind the creation story as told in the second chapter of Genesis. After God had formed man of dust from the earth, thus grounding Adam in the world of nature, He "breathed into his nostrils the breath of life; and man became a living being" (Gen. 2:7).

In the background of John's thinking may also have been Ezekiel 37. The prophet stood overlooking an ancient battlefield. Once armies had clashed there. The victor and vanquished had left their fallen dead on the desert sand. Only their bleached bones remained, and nothing is so dead as bleached bones on desert sand. No sign of life was to be seen anywhere. God spoke to the prophet, "Son of man, can these bones live?" The prophet dared not offer an opinion but simply said, "O Lord God, thou knowest" (v. 3, KJV).

Then there was a rattling up and down the valley with bones coming together, forming skeletons. Then flesh and sinew came upon the skeletons, and skin covered them. There they lay, perfectly formed bodies, but they did not live. Then God breathed His breath into them, and they stood on their feet, a mighty, living host. They lived only as God breathed His spirit and life into them.

Having given the disciples the Holy Spirit, Jesus continued: "If you forgive the sins of any, they are forgiven; if you retain the sins of any, they are retained" (v. 23). This can lend itself to a very dangerous interpretation. It must not be seen in isolation but within the context of biblical faith. That, of course, is true of all Scripture. Interpreting Scripture out of context always leads to false theology and heresy.

The Bible makes it very clear that only God can and does forgive sin. That is never a human privilege. The church, therefore, while not forgiving sin, can announce God's gracious forgiveness. It is also the painful duty of the church to declare sin unforgiven where there is no repentance and faith.

I remember the first Sundays when we observed the Lord's Supper. I stood at the table and said, "If we confess our sins, he is faithful and just, and will forgive our sins and cleanse us from all unrighteousness" (1 John 1:9). I always felt so privileged to stand there and say those gracious words. While I could not forgive sins, I was able to announce forgiveness to all who confessed their sins and trusted the grace of Christ.

The Holy Spirit gives new life to the church, clarifies its vision so it can see its mission, and empowers it so it can carry out its task. Christ sends us forth in the power of His Spirit.

I remember the Great Commission as recorded by Matthew. We see Jesus with His eleven disciples. There was not a single powerful man among them as the world understands power. He was not sending them to an adjacent town but to the nations of the world. It all seems so impossible until we see what goes before the commission and what comes after it. It is prefaced like this: "All authority in heaven and on earth has been given to me. Go therefore" (vv. 18-19). But they were not to go alone: "And lo, I am with you always, to the close of the age." Christ would go with them in the presence of the Holy Spirit.

That first Easter night, like so many great spiritual experiences, happens again. Christ comes into the midst of His tired and discouraged followers, giving them a new vision and releasing a new power into their lives. They go forth renewed in indefatigable strength. Let us set our faces in expectancy toward these Easter experiences.

Note

1. John Bunyan, *The Pilgrim's Progress* (Philadelphia: The John C. Winston Co., 1933), 73.

5
Stones that Easter Rolls Away

(Mark 16:1-8)

Some women walked through the first light of day. The darkness of the night and the heavy shadows of the early morning were being scattered. Soon the mists would be lifted from the hills and mountains. It was the most beautiful time of the day. The world seemed so clean and fresh.

These women had a problem. They were going to anoint the body of Jesus of Nazareth who just two days before had been crucified on the outskirts of the city. There was a huge stone that blocked the entrance to the tomb. How would they get in? They were asking themselves: "Who will roll away the stone for us from the door of the tomb?" (v. 3).

When they arrived, they were greatly surprised: "And looking up, they saw that the stone was rolled back—it was very large."

Easter, now as then, unblocks entrances. It rolls stones away.

Blocked Entrances

Blocked entrances are one of the great problems of life. There is a huge stone that blocks the way. It stands between where we are and where we want to be. That was the problem of those women on that first Easter morning. They wanted to do one final thing for a Person they loved very much. But a stone blocked the entrance to the tomb. Therefore, they were asking themselves: Who will roll away the stone for us?

In front of the opening of that tomb was a groove, and in the groove a circular stone as big as a cartwheel had been place. The women knew it was too much for their strength.

That is our problem, too. Blocked entrances! We would enter life, but we can't. A stone blocks the way.

Sometimes we have the sense of being trapped on the inside. We want outside, but we can't get there. The door is blocked.

Frequently we are like trapped miners. Just beyond the entrance there is light. It is a beautiful spring day with flowers blooming and birds singing, but we are cut off from the light, held in darkness. At the entrance stand family, friends, and neighbors, hoping for some good news. We would go to them, but we can't. We are trapped in our loneliness. We are captives. The pathway to light, freedom, and those we love most is blocked.

Sometimes we have the sense of standing outside, wanting to be inside. Some truth, some joy, or some relationship we would enter upon but we can't. We would go in, but we are shut out. The entrance is blocked.

It is little wonder then that Christian faith is concerned about unblocked entrances: open doors. Jesus said: "I am the door; if any one enters by me, he will be saved, and will go in and out and find pasture" (John 10:9).

John in Revelation hears God saying to the church at Philedelphia: "Behold, I have set before you an open door, which no one is able to shut" (Rev. 3:8).

There is some real sense in which this is what Easter is all about. It unblocks entrances, rolls away stones, and sets before us open doors that the mightiest powers of earth can never shut.

What Stones?

What are some of the stones that Easter rolls away?

First, the stone of weakness was removed.

You remember how weak, defeated, and frightened the first Easter found the disciples of Jesus. Just a week earlier on Palm Sunday, they appeared so jubiliant, so hopeful, and so strong. But what devastating effect seven days had had on them. The evening of the first Easter found the disciples like frightened children who had fled the streets and locked themselves behind strong doors. Jesus found them there that night. Behind locked doors! Their courage had failed them! They were a spectacle of defeat and hopelessness. They would enter upon strength again, but they couldn't. The entrance was blocked by the stone of weakness. And it was very great. But to their surprise, the stone had already been rolled away. Easter had done it.

You remember how, suddenly, their weakness was transformed into strength. The disciples walked through an open door into power, and soon they were back in those same streets from which they had fled. They were back with strength. They preached with such moving effect. Easter had released a great tide of power, and the disciples were riding the crest.

Paul tells us in the third chapter of Philippians how he turned from his own futile efforts at saving himself to Christ. He discovered power in the risen Christ. "That I may know him," Paul wrote, "and the power of his resurrection" (v. 10).

The authors of the New Testament often wrote of living in the power of the resurrection. Easter had made a difference. The risen Christ had put within their reach almost illimitable power.

The gift of the Holy Spirit was tied up with the resurrection. He was given only after the resurrection of Jesus. When the Spirit came, He came with power, like a mighty rushing wind from heaven.

How weak we often are. We know what it is to be spiritually anemic, to have our moral knees buckle beneath us. The good news is that Easter has rolled away the stone of weakness so that we can enter upon power.

Second, the stone of doubt was rolled away.

We would enter upon faith, hope, and affirmation, but the stone of doubt blocks the entrance. In our time it is very great. What will roll away the stone? Easter.

Do you remember how doubt clouded the first Easter morning? Mark tells us that when the disciples heard that Jesus had been seen by Mary Magdalene, "they would not believe it" (16:11). Luke says that when the apostles heard the good news from the women, "they did not believe them" (24:11).

Of course, Thomas is the classical example of doubt on the first Easter. John tells this story. Jesus had appeared to the disciples that night, but Thomas was absent. When Thomas found the group, they were exclaiming: "We have seen the Lord!" Thomas, being troubled with doubt, responded: "Unless I see in his hands the print of the nails, and place my finger in the mark of the nails, and place my hand in his side, I will not believe" (John 20:25).

Eight days later Jesus appeared again, and showed Thomas His hands, which still carried the prints of the nails, and His side with its wounds. In that presence, Thomas made one of the greatest confessions of the New Testament: "My Lord and my God!" (John 20:28).

The light of Easter finally drove away the clouds of doubt from the sky and rolled away the stone of doubt at the entrance of affirmation.

This Easter finds a lot of honest doubt in the minds of fine people. Like Thomas, they want to believe but can't. They see life locked in a time-space existence that blocks out the eternal dimension. Many of them are in our churches. They come wistfully, hoping that some light will fall into their lives, scattering their doubt. Let our pulpits be saying to them: "Christ is risen. We know of no reality with more convincing evidence than the resurrection of Jesus Christ. The church, the New Testament, Sunday as a day of worship, and the invincible hope in human hearts attest to the truth of Easter."

Third, the stone of guilt was taken away.

We would enter upon forgiveness, but the entrance is blocked by the stone of guilt. It is very great. What will roll it away? Easter.

Forgiveness is inextricably linked to the resurrection. "If Christ has not been raised," Paul writes, "your faith is futile and you are still in your sins" (1 Cor. 15:17).

What sobering words are these: "You are still in your sins." If Christ was left in His tomb, obviously He was the victim of evil forces. How then can a dead Christ forgive the guilt that evil and sin made inevitable? He can't. But Christ is risen! In His resurrection, He not only mastered death but also the evil that was responsible for His death. He who has overcome evil is certainly able to forgive the sin and guilt that evil has caused.

One of the most interesting exhibits at the Protestant and Orthodox center of the World's Fair in New York City during the middle 1960s was the Charred Cross of Coventry. The Nazi bombers in destroying the city had not spared its beautiful cathedral. After its destruction, a workman salvaged a burned cross and bound it together with metal bands. Somebody wrote "Father forgive" across the charred cross which was placed in the destroyed cathedral. Why write *forgive* across the face of Christ's cross if He is still in His tomb? That would make no sense at all. But since He is risen, write that wonderful word boldly across His cross.

In the first chapter of Revelation, there is a beautiful, hymn that is ascribes praise to our risen Lord: "To him who loves us and has freed us from our sins by his blood and made us a kingdom, priests to his God and Father, to him be glory and dominion for ever and ever. Amen" (1:5-6).

The risen Christ has freed us from our sins by His own blood. Therefore, He is able to roll away the stone that blocks our path into forgiveness.

But we should remember that our being forgiven is related to our willingness to forgive. Jesus said if we do not forgive men their trespasses, our Father will not forgive us. This does not mean that we earn God's forgiveness by forgiving our brothers. But it does mean that by our willingness to forgive we unclutter our lives and open them to the forgiveness of God.

A beautiful story about a Belgian girl came from World War II. Nazi bombers had destroyed much of her town and killed some of her friends. She went into her church which lay in partial ruins. The roof was caved in, and the beautiful windows lay in broken pieces on the floor. She knelt at the altar which was split in half and began to pray the Lord's Prayer. When she tried to say "as we forgive" (Matt. 6:12, KJV), she choked on the word *forgive*. How could she forgive her enemies who had bombed her town, killed her friends, and left her church in shambles. The girl tried again and failed. The third time she was no more successful. She would make a final effort. And when the girl came to the great hurdle, a voice from behind her led her on—"as we forgive those who trespass against us"—and continued to the end. The girl turned to see who the gentle man was who had given her courage, and standing behind her was the King of Belgium.

Just so with us. We find it hard to forgive. And when we are struggling to say that hard word, our risen King leads us on: "Go ahead and say it. As you forgive, I will forgive you." We forgive and in turn are forgiven.

Fourth, the stone of death has been removed.

We would enter upon life, but the stone of death blocks the entrance. The stone is very great. It is more than a stone, it is a boulder that blocks the entrance to life. Who will roll it away? Easter will.

Here we are at the heart of Easter faith. Easter concerns death—your death, the death of your child, and everyone's death—and Easter concerns life—your life, the life of your friend, the life of every person. It opens the door to the life everlasting.

Yet, death seems to be so final. The voice that was so vibrant just a few hours ago is now so silent; the face that was so expressive is now vacant; the hand that was so warm is now cold; the life that was so active is now so still. Death seems to be the end.

A soldier during World War II, who for months had lived amid death, struck a match, blew it out, and said to his chaplain: "Isn't that what happens at death, Chaplain?" It is easy to be cynical about any life beyond this one.

But Easter will not come to terms with any shallow cynicism about life. It affirms life. It says that the boulder of death has been pushed from the doorway into eternal life by the risen Christ.

Famous journalist William Allen White lost his daughter, Mary, while she was a high-school student. Her spirited horse ran beneath a tree limb, and Mary died from the injury she suffered. After her death, her father wrote an editorial about her that appeared in *The Emporia Gazette*, a famous newspaper he edited. White told of Mary's love for life, her vivacious spirit, her sense of fairness and equality, and her compassion for people. He closed his editorial with reference to her casket as it was lowered into the grave:

> A rift in the clouds in a gray day threw a shaft of sunlight upon the coffin as her nervous energetic little body sank to its sleep. But the soul

of her, the flowing, gorgeous, fervent soul of her, surely was flaming in eager joy upon some other dawn.

We can write with that kind of hope with confidence if we believe that Easter has rolled away the stone of death at the entrance of life.

So Easter comes again to us where we are trapped, assuring us that the way to strength, faith, forgiveness, and life has been unblocked. The stone at the tomb, which was very great, has been rolled away.

6
The Person of Easter

(Matt. 28:1-10; Rev. 1:17-20)

Christianity is about a person, the Person of Easter. It is not an ideology although it makes wide use of ideas. It is not about ideals, yet it possesses some of the most beautiful in the world. It is not about a system of thought although it writes systematic theologies. It is not about a way of life, however it points in the way we should go. It is about a Person.

We sometimes say that Christ is Christianity. You would never say that about the founders of other great religions of our world. You would never say that Moses is Judaism, that Confucious is Confucianism, nor that Muhammad is Islam. About Christ alone do we say that kind of thing.

Matthew in his Easter story tells what an awe-inspiring Person the resurrected Lord is. Christ met a group of women on that first Easter morning and greeted them. They took hold of His feet and worshiped Him.

John in the first chapter of Revelation gives us an even more awesome picture of the risen Christ. He stands in regal splendor. He is a mighty Conqueror with the keys of "Death and Hades" dangling from His waist. Yet, He is very human, having lived and died.

Power Touched with Gentleness

John tells us that when He saw the risen Christ, He fell at His feet as one dead. There was a terrifying majesty about Him. Yet Christ was not casual and aloof. He moved quickly to the prostrate man, laid His right hand on him, and said, "Fear not" (v. 17).

We see the unbroken continuity between Jesus of Nazareth and the risen Christ. He has stood on the other side of the grave, but He is the same Person. He shows the same love, mercy, and caring. Jesus was always moved by the pain, loneliness, and fear in the lives of others. His compassion ran even through His hands and fingers. He was always touching somebody, even the untouchables. He knew we are not disembodied spirits. He was aware that there was comfort and healing in the physical touch. The Gospel writers often tell stories about the therapy of touch.

A leper came to Jesus one day and kneeling before Him, said, "Lord, if you will, you can make me clean." A leper was a most pitiable character. He lived beyond the walls of the town away from family and friends. His social stigma was great. His loneliness and separation were almost unbearable. When a leper approached anyone, he cried, "Unclean! Unclean!" And when a person talked with a leper, he or she had to keep a safe distance of six feet.

In response to the leper's plea, Jesus stretched out His hand and touched him, saying, "I will; be clean" (Matt. 8:3). He touched a leper who was an untouchable.

The transfiguration reminds us of our Scripture lesson. The disciples were overcome by wonder and awe and fell on their faces. Jesus came to them, touched them, and said, "Rise, and have no fear" (Matt. 17:7).

Jesus' mighty power was tempered by gentleness and mercy. Jesus showed us how to use power. He was not ruthless, careless, and irresponsible. He was gentle and socially responsible.

How do you use power? That is certainly one of the most important of all human questions. The misuse of power explains so much of the tragedy of life. Unless power lies in hands that are gentle and socially responsible, it can be very destructive. At no time in history has the use of power been so crucially important as now. In a nuclear age, if power gets into the wrong hands, life—all life—can be destroyed on our planet.

Alive for Evermore

Christ has lived, died, and is now alive forevermore. "I died," He told John, "and beyond I am alive for evermore."

He is no phantom from another world. In a basic sense, He is one of us. He is human.

We should not forget that Jesus lived the kind of life we do. He knew what it was to become tired, need food and rest, and get up refreshed in the morning. He played, laughed, went to parties, and had fun. He knew what it was to hope, wonder, and dream. He needed and wanted friends, especially in lonely hours. He knew what it was to be depressed, to have heavy shadows lie across His mind. We see Him in the garden of Gethsemane with sweat, like drops of blood, falling from His forehead to the ground. His cry of dereliction from the cross, "My God, my God, why hast thou forsaken me?" (Mark 15:34) was in part the cry of a depressed man. His temptation in the wilderness was not shadowboxing. It was not acting and pretending. It was the real thing.

He died the way all of us do. If the blood that flowed from His wounds on that fateful day had been put under chemical analysis, it would have been the same kind of blood that flows through your veins and mine.

Though like us in many ways, He was also different from us. He was not the victim of His tomb the way you and I are. He came out of it victorious and triumphant on Easter morning.

He is alive forevermore. Having died, He will not die again. He is now beyond the powerful coalition of church and state. He is now beyond the reach of governor, priest, and Roman soldier. He will never have another nail driven into His hands nor another sword pierce His side. He will never have to die again the humiliating death of a Roman cross. He has gone free of death, and death can never overtake Him again.

Paul wrote: "For we know that Christ being raised from the dead will never die again; death no longer has dominion over him. The death he died he died to sin, once for all, but the life he lives he lives to God" (Rom. 6:9-10).

This is such a wonderful verse of Scripture. Let us hear it again from other translations. "For we know that Christ has been raised from death and will never die again—death will no longer rule over him. And so, because he died, sin has no power over him; and now he lives his life in fellowship with God" (GNB).

"We can be sure that the risen Christ never dies again—death's power to master him is finished. He died, because of sin, once: he lives for God for ever" (Phillips).

These translations have fresh nuances of thought, but they are saying the same thing. And it is wonderful!

A Title Like God's

In this awesome experience John had with the resurrected Lord, Christ says of Himself: "I am the first and the last" (v. 17). It is like the title given to God.

God speaks of Himself like this: "'I am the Alpha and the Omega', says the Lord God, who is and who was and who is to come" (Rev. 1:8). That is the way Christ speaks of Himself. Like God, Jesus is the first and the last; He stands at the beginning and will stand at the end.

In Jesus you are confronted with no ordinary person. He is a Person who comes from God, speaks for God, and reveals God. He has pulled back the curtain that hid God so that we can behold His face. He does those things that only God can do. He is Immanuel: God with us.

The purpose of the Book of Hebrews is to show the superiority and uniqueness of Jesus Christ. His likeness had never been seen before and will never be seen again. He is the only one of His kind. At the very beginning of his book the author points to the absolute uniqueness of Jesus Christ:

> In these last days he has spoken to us by a Son, whom he appointed the heir of all things, through whom also he created the world. He reflects the glory of God and bears the very stamp of his nature, upholding the universe by his word of power. When he had made purification for sins, he sat down at the right hand of the Majesty on high (Heb. 1:2-3).

Then the author takes up the basic tenets of the Hebrew faith one by one and shows how Christ is superior to each and all of them.

The author began with angels. Jesus Christ is pictured as Creator, something angels could never be. He will outlast His temporal creation: "They will perish, but thou remainest; / they will all grow old like a garment, / like a mantle thou wilt roll them up, / and they will be changed. / But thou art the same, / and thy years will never end" (Heb. 1:11-12).

Jesus Christ stood with God in the early morning of creation. "I am the first." He saw the darkness and chaos of things. Then matter began to take form, and creation got underway. The heavens were created, and land with the seas appeared. Next came life: plant life, animal life, and, finally, regal creatures appeared called human beings. They were especially gifted by God and would be the keepers of God's creation.

Christ will stand at the end of time. "I am the . . . last." History moves to an end, and Christ will be there to consummate it. He will judge the nations of earth, and history will be at an end.

Jesus tells about the end in Matthew 25, known as the parable of the last judgment. He introduces it like this:

> When the Son of man comes in his glory, and all the angels with him, then he will sit on his glorious throne. Before him will be gathered all the nations, and he will separate them one from another as a shepherd separates the sheep from the goats. (v. 31).

I am never prepared to hear what that parable says. I am surprised, sometimes shocked.

When I remember Jesus as a servant, I am surprised to see Him as a King. When I see a scepter in His hand which He once rejected for a towel and basin of water, I am surprised.

I am surprised that the poor, the hungry, the homeless, and the disenfranchised of our earth are so prominent. They will be the witnesses. They are not the kind of witnesses I would have chosen. I would have selected middle-class people, fine, successful, cultured persons. I would have chosen my kind.

There are so many poor, helpless, hungry homeless people in my time. In our shrunken world they are so close to me. Their paths intersect mine in strange and unexpected ways. They are so near that they almost press their pinched faces against the window panes of my dining room, looking in upon my table laden with rich and abundant food. They reach toward me, almost being able to touch my face with their thin bony fingers. I cannot escape them now, and Jesus said I cannot escape them in the judgment.

I am surprised at the questions that will be asked. I would have expected biblical and theological ones, but basically they are social questions. Did you feed the hungry? Did you take in the homeless? Did you visit the sick? Did you care about prisoners?

Yet, nothing is said about their being saved by humanitarian deeds. They have been saved the way all of us are—by grace.

I am surprised by what Jesus said about Himself. Before Him were the poor, hungry, homeless, sick, and prisoners. Yet, Jesus did not say they were poor, hungry, homeless, sick, and prisoners, but that He was. He was poor, hungry, homeless, sick, and imprisoned.

That sounds so strange. What could it possibly mean? It means that He was so identified with them that their poverty, hunger, homelessness, sickness, and imprisonment became His own.

A Mighty Conqueror

Jesus Christ is the mighty Conqueror. There is nothing weak, vacillating, and indecisive about Him. He who has known the weakness of men now knows the power of God.

He looks so different than He did on Good Friday when He stumbled beneath His cross through the streets of jeering people. There is nothing about Him now that reminds us of His slow, painful death and His limp body on a Roman cross. He is the essence of strength and power.

As a symbol of His authority and power, Jesus wears the keys of "Death and Hades." He who wears the keys unlocks the doors that are closed to others; He goes and comes as He wills.

This was particularly impressive to John who was a prisoner on the Isle of Patmos, separated from his family and churches on the mainland. He knew what it was to be denied freedom, to have clanking chains around his ankles, and to be locked behind prison bars. Before him was the risen Christ who could never be put behind prison walls again. He has access to entrances that are closed to others.

The risen Christ is a person of authority. He speaks words that other men and women are to obey; He has power others cannot command.

The risen Christ has the keys to death which is our last and most formidable enemy. All of us win skirmishes with death, but we know who wins the last great battle—death does. Death locks us in a tomb that is a prison from which none of us can escape.

Death seems so final. Yet, Christian faith will not have it so. It does not believe that dust is the end of life. It knows that the dates cut on tombstones cannot tell the whole story about our lives. Death, rather than being the end, is a doorway. There is more beyond.

The risen Christ holds not only the keys to death but hades as well. Hades is the abode of the dead. Christ has not only dealt a mortal blow to death, but He has also conquered Hades.

This is God's universe, and nothing is off limits to Him. God did not create the universe and then get locked out of it. The psalmist believed that he could not escape God's presence since He is everywhere in his Spirit. He could say, "If I ascend to heaven, thou art there! / If I make my bed in Sheol, thou art there!" (Ps. 139:8). (*Sheol* is roughly the Hebrew equivalent of the Greek hades. It is where the Hebrews believed people went after death.)

There are no off limits in our universe to the living Christ. Not even hades is beyond the boundary of His providence and grace.

There are several interesting passages in the New Testament that speak of Christ in His relations to hades, especially 1 Peter 3:18-20:

> For Christ also died for sins once for all, the righteous for the unrighteous, that he might bring us to God, being put to death in the flesh but made alive in the spirit; in which he went and preached to the spirits in prison, who formerly did not obey, when God's patience waited in the days of Noah, during the building of the ark, in which a few, that is eight persons, were saved through water.

Peter believed that Christ, sometime between His death and res-urrection, descended into Hades and preached to the prisoners there.

The tradition of Christ's descent into hell early became a part of the church's theology and was expressed in some of its creeds. The Apostle's Creed says, "He descended into hell."

We would not want to be dogmatic in the interpretation of this passage. Yet, one thing is clear: Hell is not beyond the domain of our risen Christ. He holds the keys to hades.

The ultimate issues of life, death, and hell are in the hands of our risen Christ. We can trust Him! Let us therefore step into the future unafraid.

7

The Power
of His Resurrection

(Phil. 3:1-10)

I am thinking of four lovely chapel windows which are abstract art. There is not a clearly defined symbol or subject in any of the windows. Yet, one of them is known as the resurrection window. It has beautiful rectangular bars of roughly-cut colored glass. The pattern is broken. Those bars of glass abut each other at odd angles. Everything seems to be in disarray. There is upheaval as if the stones have been hit by something like an earthquake.

We can understand why the window is called the resurrection window. Easter knows a power greater than an earthquake. We can understand the meaning of Paul's words: "That I may know him and the power of his resurrection" (v. 10).

Resurrection as Power

The resurrection of Jesus is power in at least three senses.

First, it is an event of power. Something of tremendous power happened on Easter morning. Earth's most impregnable prison, the tomb, had its bars borne away. A heavy stone, blocking the entrance to the sepulcher, was rolled away. A man went forth from the grave, leaving His shroud behind Him. Light more powerful than that of the sun shone, and continues to shine from that Easter morning. The power of Easter shook a drowsy and despairing world, giving it hope. Doors to life, which we could not open, have been shaken ajar by the resurrection of Jesus.

The power of Easter is not something impersonal and far removed from us. It speaks to us personally as well walk in the shadows of our mortality. It speaks about those we have loved and lost and about those we will someday have to lose. The power of the resurrection can be very comforting and healing.

Rufus Jones, a great mystic of a generation ago, was on an ocean voyage and, while on the mid-Atlantic, got a cablegram that his seventeen-year-old son, Lowell, was critically ill. Before he could get home, the boy had died. Jones became very depressed, and for several months walked in a deep shadow that would not be lifted. The depression, however, passed one day when he saw a little girl struggling to open a gate into a garden. She tried desperately to get in, but she could not. The harder she tried the more fretted she became. Then the door was opened, and the voice of her mother was heard: "Didn't you know I would open it from the other side?"

Yet, the power of Easter as event is not loud, ruthless, and overwhelming. It is like the sunrise. There is no blast in the east, no sound of a trumpet, no bugle announcing the morning. The sun quietly spills its energy and pours its light over our world giving warmth and life. But the resurrection is personal in a way the sunrise never can be. It is almost as if a voice from that early morning speaks, calling us by name. It speaks to our sorrow and grief, our sense of loss, and our anxieties about death. It speaks about life's ultimate meaning.

Second, the resurrection has released a Person of power. It has released Jesus Christ who is now beyond and free of all powers that would bind and enslave Him.

E. L. Doctorow tells about Harry Houdini in his book *Ragtime*. Houdini, as the world knows, was a headliner in the top vaudeville circuits more than fifty years ago. His audiences were made up of ordinary people: peddlers, policemen, and children. His life seemed absurd as he went all over the world subjecting himself to all kinds of bondage. Yet he always escaped. He was roped to a chair and chained to a ladder. He escaped. He was handcuffed, his legs put in irons tied up in a straitjacket, and placed in a locked cabinet. He escaped. He freed himself from bank vaults, nailed-up barrels, and sewn mailbags; he escaped from a zinc-lined piano case, a giant football, a galvanized iron boiler, a rolltop desk, and a sausage skin. Houdini's escapes were mystifying since he never damaged nor appeared to unlock what he escaped from. When the screen was removed, there he stood, cool and triumphant beside the inviolable container that was supposed to have imprisoned him. He waved to the crowd who cheered him.

Finally, Houdini was buried alive in a grave but this time he could not escape. He had to be rescued. Hurriedly they dug him out, "The earth is too heavy," he said, grasping for breath. His nails bled, and soil fell from his eyes. He was pale, and he couldn't stand up. Houdini wheezed, sputtered, and coughed blood. His assistants cleaned him off and took him back to his hotel.

Houdini escaped from seemingly invincible prisons and impregnable strongholds. He always came out cool and confident, waving his hands in triumph. But there was a prison from which Houdini could not escape. Jesus Christ, however, on Easter morning, went free from something more powerful than a grave. He went free of death itself.

John in Revelation pictures Jesus Christ as the risen Lord, far more triumphant than Houdini ever was. From Christ's waist were dangling the keys of death and hell, and He was saying: "Fear not, I am first and the last, and the living one; I died, and beyond I am alive for evermore, and I have the keys of Death and Hades" (1:17-18).

When Paul thought of Jesus, he first looked at the past. Jesus was a historical Person. His life was dated. But it was not enough to remember and keep glancing back over his shoulder at that towering personality. Christ was alive; He was in some real sense Paul's great contemporary.

Paul believed that the death of Jesus reconciled men and women to God, but it was by His resurrected life that He saved them. "For if while we were enemies we were reconciled to God by the death of his Son," Paul wrote, "much more, now that we are reconciled, shall we be saved by his life" (Rom. 5:10). The cross was like a magnet, pulling estranged and faraway people back to God in peace and reconciliation. But Christ was saving them through the power of His present life.

In knowing the living Christ, Paul wanted to experience the power of His resurrection. And this he did. What a powerful man Paul became. We see this little man tramping across two continents, shaking them to their foundations. If you had asked him the secret of his power, he certainly would not have pointed to himself, gifted as he was. He would have pointed to his resurrected Lord.

Third, the resurrection of Jesus is related to a presence of power: the Holy Spirit.

Jesus, on the eve of leaving His disciples, promised to send them another Comforter or counselor who would always be with them. He could not stay with them, but the Comforter would not leave them, abiding with them forever. He would always be by their sides, giving strength and guidance, and helping them to remember Jesus. Nothing could ever take the Comforter away from them.

But as you recall, the Comforter or Holy Spirit was not given until after the resurrection. It would be the resurrected Christ who would send the Spirit. And when He came, He came as power, the way Jesus said He would. "But you shall receive power when the Holy Spirit has come upon you" (Acts 1:8). When He came upon the early church at Pentecost, the Spirit came "like the rush of a mighty wind" (2:2).

Paul said the same Spirit that raised Jesus Christ from the dead was working in the lives of His followers. This is one of the most startling things in the New Testament. There was resurrection power in the disciples. "If the Spirit of him who raised Jesus from the dead dwells in you," Paul wrote, "he who raised Christ Jesus from the dead will give life to your mortal bodies also through his Spirit which dwells in you" (Rom. 8:11).

Again Paul speaks of the "immeasurable greatness of his power in us who believe, according to the working of his great might which he accomplished in Christ when he raised him from the dead" (Eph. 1:19-20). It was the Spirit that transferred the power of the resurrection into the lives of Christians, saving them from their weaknesses and giving them power out of all proportion to their numbers.

Power Still Available

It is good to remember on Easter that this power is available to us. It has never been dissipated, wasted, or used up. It is fed by unfailing and imperishable sources of strength and life. Therefore, if Easter finds you weak and vacillating you don't have to stay that way. Power is available.

Are your moral knees buckling beneath you? Is some evil habit forging manacles which one day will enslave you? Are there forces of hatred, hostility, and anger in you which you dread? Are you afraid that someday they, like a volcano, will erupt to destroy you? Are there broken relationships with important people in your life that leave you hurt and lonely? Does God seem far away and unavailable? Are you anxious about life, the future, and death? If so, take heart: There is hope in "him and the power of his resurrection." The living Christ is still saving us, healing us, pouring His love into our hearts by the Holy Spirit, striking chains that would enslave us, and empowering us.

Commander Mitsuo Fuchida led the Japanese attack on Pearl Harbor with its destructive and far-reaching effect. Hating Americans, Fuchida became more bitter after we dropped the atomic bombs on Hiroshima and Nagasaki. His hatred was further enflamed when he was led to believe that Americans, like Japanese, tortured their prisoners. But Fuchida had some positive exposure to Christians and Christian influence. One day when his anger and hatred were about to destroy him, and he was in great desperation, he said to himself: *Maybe a Bible could help me.* He began reading a Japanese translation. He later declared that when he came to Luke 23 and read Christ's prayer just before He died on the cross, then he understood. "I met Jesus that day. . . . He came into my heart and changed my life from a military officer to a warrior for Christ." Mitsuo Fuchida became a great preacher of the gospel of Christ.[1]

Note

1. Chevis F. Horne, *Dynamic Preaching* (Broadman Press, 1983), 40-41.

8
Through Doubt to Faith

(John 20:24-29)

We walk through the darkness of night into the light of morning. We often walk through the shadows of doubt into the light of faith. Such was Thomas's experience a week after Easter.

Thomas had not been with the other disciples when Jesus appeared to them on Easter night. When Thomas joined them, he found them saying in a kind of ecstasy: "We have seen the Lord"! But Thomas was not convinced. "Unless I see in his hands the print of the nails," he said, "and place my finger in the mark of the nails, and place my hand in his side, I will not believe" (v. 25).

Then a week later, with Thomas present, Jesus appeared in the midst of His disciples. Again came the familiar greeting, "Peace be with you" (v. 26). Then Jesus showed Thomas His hands that had been pierced with Roman nails and His side that had been wounded by a Roman sword. Thomas believed! He made the greatest confession found anywhere in the New Testament: "My Lord and my God!" (v. 28).

A Quest for Experience

Here we find one of the great themes of John's Gospel—experience. You are invited to see, feel, handle, and experience spiritual reality. The theme is introduced early. In the first chapter, two of John the Baptist's disciples followed Jesus. Jesus turning and seeing them, asked: "What do you seek?" They responded, "Rabbi, . . . where are you staying?" And Jesus said to them, "Come and see" (vv. 37-39). He didn't give them instructions as to how to find Him. He invited them to come and find out for themselves.

The Samaritan men said, after the woman had told them about
Jesus, "It is no longer because of your words that we believe, for we
have heard for ourselves, and we know that this is indeed the Savior
of the world" (John 4:42). The man blind from birth, whom Jesus
healed, when pressed by the Pharisees responded, "Whether he is a
sinner, I do not know; one thing I know, that though I was blind,
now I see" (John 9:25).

When Jesus was on trial before Pilate, the governor asked him:
"Are you the King of the Jews?" Once more Jesus appealed to personal knowledge and experience: "Do you say this of your own ac-
cord," He asked, "or did others say it to you about me?" (John
18:34).

In our Scripture lesson today we are introduced again to this
theme in a very dramatic, even bizarre, sort of way. Thomas, not
satisfied with what others were saying about the resurrected Lord,
strongly asserted that he must see and know for himself: "Unless I
see in his hands the print of the nails, and place my finger in the
mark of the nails, and place my hand in his side, I will not believe"
(v. 25).

It becomes obvious that running through the New Testament is
this quest for firsthand, personal experience.

The reality of personal experience and the urgency of witnessing
are coupled together. Jesus made this very clear when He said to
Nicodemus: "We speak of what we know, and bear witness to what
we have seen" (John 3:11).

The disciples of Jesus were not to go into the world with theory
and speculation. They were to go as witnesses, telling what they had
experienced. They were to tell what their hands had handled, their
eyes had seen, their ears had heard, and their hearts had felt. John,
in his first letter, put it this way: "That which was from the beginning, which we have heard, which we have seen with our eyes,
which we have looked upon and touched with our hands, concerning the word of life . . . we proclaim also to you" (1 John 1:1-3).

The world still wants that kind of witnessing. A bright, cynical
mind may point out problems connected with Christianity. But
there is no argument against a person who knows what he believes,

whose heart has become serene in his faith, who has unshakable foundations beneath his feet, and whose life of love issues in service that binds up wounds and enables people to stand to their feet in self-respect and dignity. The world still needs, and, in its best moments, wants that kind of witness.

The Reality of Doubt

In our story we find both faith and doubt. Yet, there should be nothing strange about that. How often they walk side by side and go hand in hand. They make strange bedfellows, but how often we find them in the same bed. Many of us know what it is to doubt and believe at the same time.

Life is often like a jigsaw puzzle. All the pieces do not fit together. Try as hard as we may, there are some odd pieces that will not help form a pattern. In such experiences, we may wonder about the meaning of life. It doesn't seem to make sense.

Jesus was never severe on a person besieged by doubt. He was not hard on Thomas. Jesus did not say to him: "I am shocked by your doubt, Thomas. You have been one of My disciples, and I have expected better things of you." He was very gentle and affirming. He simply said to him: "Put your finger here, and see my hands; and put out your hand, and place it in my side; do not be faithless, but believing" (v. 27).

Do you remember how gentle Jesus was with the father of the boy with the deaf and dumb spirit? The boy had suffered much, but the father had suffered more. The father came to Jesus half believing and half doubting. "If you can do anything," he said, "have pity on us and help us" (Mark 9:22). He was saying in effect: "I am not sure You can do anything, but if You can please help us." And Jesus was not severe on him. Jesus responded: "If you can! All things are possible to him who believes." And the father confessing his ambivalence said: "I believe; help my unbelief!" (Mark 9:24).

We can learn a lot from Jesus. We do not help a person overcome doubts by being harsh and censorious but by creating a relationship that encourages faith and trust. This is what Jesus did.

Thomas depicted the modern mind more than anybody in the

New Testament. His doubt was the kind men and women experience today. He wanted to be able to see, touch, and handle. He wanted to be able to weigh, measure, and prove. He wanted a logical and rational approach to reality. Many in our modern world can identify with Thomas.

Our job is not to condemn and reject. We are to accept in loving care those who find it hard to believe, and we are to exercise a faith that is winsome and contagious. We must all know that we do not overcome doubt in others by outarguing them but by outloving and outliving them.

One more observation must be made about doubt: in some cases, doubt is not the enemy of faith but its friend. How can that be?

Religion can be more vulnerable to superstition and irrationality than anything I know. We do such foolish, ridiculous, and destructive things in the name of God. For example, here are parents who let their child die, refusing on religious grounds to go to a doctor. Or, here is a man who is a member of a snake-handling cult and is fatally bitten by a rattler. But did not Jesus say, "They will pick up serpents, and if they drink any deadly thing, it will not hurt them" (Mark 16:18)? These are dramatic examples of what can happen to persons, but also many people have their religion infused with a milder form of superstition and irrationality.

Here is where doubt can play a very important role. It can call into question those practices that are either irrational or unchristian. In so doing, doubt becomes the friend of authentic faith.

Religion may take into itself many extraneous things that become like thick, high underbrush that hides the trees, the morning light, and the stars that come out at night. Here doubt, armed with more rational tools, can help cut away the underbrush, letting the light shine through.

A Great Confession of Faith

When Thomas saw the hands and side of Christ, he gave a great exclamation of faith: "My Lord and my God!" There are many confessions of faith in the New Testament, but this is the greatest of them all. This confession of faith is more comprehensive, more personal, and filled with greater feeling and passion than any of the rest.

My Lord! Jesus Christ is Lord. That was the earliest Christian confession of faith. When the early church members made that confession of faith, they knew they were speaking about One to whom they belonged, who had delivered them from bondage into freedom, and who alone was worthy of controlling and directing their lives. But was not He the one, who refusing a crown, asked for a towel and basin of water? Did He not wash and dry the dirty feet of men? Was not He best known as servant? How then could He be Lord?

This was no problem for the early church. Christ was both servant and Lord. The people held these two roles together in their worship. They sang of His being on an equality with God, a position He did not have to force, filch, or steal. It really belonged to Him. Then He freely gave it all up and made a radical descent into our sinful world. Jesus came way down. He became a man, lower still, a servant man, and lowest of all, He died the most shameful death of the ancient world: He died as a felon on a Roman cross. Then He made an ascent as steep as the descent. God highly exalted Him, giving Him a name above all other names. At last, "at the name of Jesus every knee should bow, in heaven, and on earth, and under the earth, and every tongue confess that Jesus Christ is Lord, to the glory of God the Father." The early Christians felt no tension in the two images. The love that made Christ servant also made Him Lord. (See Phil. 2:5-11.)

My God! That is possibly the most radical thing ever said about Jesus Christ. None of the other confessions are so radical. Yet, this extravagant claim is a part of the New Testament faith about Jesus Christ.

John in the prologue to his Gospel says that Jesus was the Word whom he equates with God. He introduced his prologue like this: "In the beginning was the Word, and the Word was with God, and the Word was God" (1:1). Then "the Word became flesh and dwelt among us" (v. 14).

Paul in Colossians speaks of Christ like this:

He is the image of the invisible God, the first-born of all creation; . . .
For in him all the fulness of God was pleased to dwell, and through
him to reconcile in himself all things, whether on earth or in heaven,
making peace by the blood of his cross (1:15,19-20).

Maybe our best gift to this world is nothing more or less than
making Thomas's confession and allowing it to transform our lives.
Others who find it hard to believe can be encouraged and chal-
lenged by our faith until they are able to believe for themselves.

Dr. Harris Kirk was a Presbyterian minister who for many years
served a church in Baltimore, Maryland. He had fine intellectual
powers and integrity that inspired trust in people. He was spoken of
as the best-read person in the American pulpit. A professor from
Johns Hopkins University, who found faith difficult, was regularly
in Dr. Kirk's congregation. He said to Dr. Kirk one day; "Dr. Kirk I
cannot believe, but you can, and you are an intelligent man with
unquestioned integrity. I hope to believe some day."

Trusting the Invisible

After Thomas made his great confession, Jesus said to him: "Have
you believed because you have seen me? Blessed are those who have
not seen and yet believe."

Thomas wanted proof. He desired to see the risen Lord, to put his
finger in the prints of His hands and his hand in the wound of His
side. The fact he could see the risen Christ and touch Him convinced Thomas of the reality of the resurrection. But what would
happen to his faith when Jesus would no longer be visibly present?

Here is one of the weaknesses of religion for most people. We
want visible signs that tell us where God is and what He is doing.
We want to see the spectacular and dramatic that point to God.

We had a religious group in our city several years ago. They were
people of great grace and acceptance. Their doors were always open
to anyone who needed help regardless of race or class. No one was
ever turned away. But they appealed to the spectacular. It was
widely told that they prayed for people who had one leg shorter than
the other, and as they prayed one could see the short leg growing.

That seemed to impress people more than the grace that was unmistakably present in their lives. Jesus discouraged that kind of thing. "Blessed are those who have not seen and yet believe" (v. 29).

Biblical faith places its emphasis not on the seen but on the unseen, not on the visible but on the invisible.

We believe that our physical world can never explain itself. It is explained by an unseen world that impinges on it and intersects its time. It is as if the stream of eternity washes our shores of time.

Paul could say: "We look not to the things that are seen but to the things that are unseen; for the things that are seen are transient, but the things that are unseen are eternal" (2 Cor. 4:18).

In the early experience of Easter the empty tomb was pointed to as proof of the resurrection. But the focus began to shift from the empty tomb to the risen Christ, from the sign of the resurrection to the reality of it. Paul never mentioned the empty tomb, yet he was so aware of the unseen but resurrected Lord.

Israel's God was unseen and invisible. Her sanctuaries were bare. No statuary, images, or paintings were allowed. These would tempt the people to believe that God was visible.

When Jesus left, the Holy Spirit was given. Jesus said He would be unseen and intangible. He would be like the wind that "blows where it wills, and you hear the sound of it, but you do not know whence it comes or whither it goes" (John 3:8).

The writer of the Hebrews tells of the great heroes of his nation's past. What a company of people! The world was not worthy of them. He said of Moses that "he endured as seeing him who is invisible" (11:27). That could have been said of all those noble people.

The last promise Jesus made His disciples was, "Lo, I am with you always, to the close of the age" (Matt. 28:20). He would be an unseen traveler going their way.

David Livingstone, just before he sailed to Africa, claimed this promise of Jesus, believing that His words were the words of a gentleman. If Jesus made the promise, He would keep it. Years later Livingstone told a college audience that Jesus had been as good as His word, an unseen friend tramped beside Him every step of the way across that unexplored continent.

Many people believe that Phillips Brooks was the greatest preacher America has produced. He was for several years rector of Trinity Episcopal Church in Boston. I had for years wanted to attend the church. In 1942 and again in 1979, I visited Trinity Church. Both times the really significant experience didn't happen inside the sanctuary but on the lawn as I stood before a life-sized statue of Brooks. The statue stands on a pedestal, under a half dome within a portico. On the base of the statue are these words: "Phillips Brooks—Preacher of the Word of God, Lover of mankind." Brooks is standing to the right side of his pulpit, his left arm resting on it. His right hand is raised as if to speak. Towering above Brooks is the living Christ with His right hand resting on Brook's left shoulder. It is as if Christ is saying: "Go ahead, Brooks, and speak the Word, I am with you." If Christ has promised to go with us to the end of the age, he will certainly go with us into our pulpits![1]

Maybe we cannot escape doubt. But let us not linger too long in its shadows. Let us walk resolutely toward the light of faith.

Note

1. Chevis F. Horne, *Dynamic Preaching* (Nashville: Broadman Press, 1983), 135.

9
Easter Transformations

(Mark 16:1-6; 1 Cor. 15:54-58)

Easter changes things, and always for the better. It takes the shameful and turns it into glory, the marred and makes it beautiful. It takes despair and turns it into hope, the weak and makes it strong. It takes the shadows of night and turns them into the brightness of morning. It takes death and turns it into life. Easter transforms. Therefore, we can speak of Easter transformation.

Halford E. Luccock says about Easter:

> He is risen. These three words form the greatest watershed of history. Everything that has flowed from them—the creation of the Christian Church, the Gospel of the resurrection with which it went into the world, the Christian experience of the living Christ, the new valuation which the Resurrection put upon man—all these bear witness to the reality and transforming power of the event itself.

What is it Easter transforms?

Things

We are surrounded by things, and Easter's transforming power is felt here. I mention two of these in particular: a cross and a tomb.

The cross in the time of Jesus was an extremely torturous and shameful instrument of death. No Roman citizen was ever allowed to die on it. The worst Roman citizen was too good for that. It was reserved for foreigners, slaves, and insurrectionists. When Paul says that Jesus became "obedient unto death, even death on a cross," he means that Jesus died the most shameful death of the ancient world. When early Christians confessed that their Lord had died on a cross, the response was usually negative. Paul describes the reaction to the cross like this: "For Jews demand signs and Greeks seek wisdom, but we preach Christ crucified, a stumbling block to Jews and folly to Gentiles" (1 Cor. 1:22-23).

But the light of Easter morning transformed and transfigured the cross for the believers in Jesus. Its stigma had been removed, its shame had been lifted. It was no longer shame but glory, no longer weakness but strength. It stood as a symbol of God's victory over sin, the place where men and women could be saved.

Paul, therefore, could say: "For the word of the cross is folly to those who are perishing, but to us who are being saved it is the power of God" (1 Cor. 1:18). Or again, "I decided to know nothing among you except Jesus Christ and him crucified" (1 Cor 2:2). Hear Paul again: "But far be it from me to glory except in the cross of our Lord Jesus Christ" (Gal. 6:14).

Easter transformed the cross into a thing of glory. We sing: "In the cross of Christ I glory, / Towr'ing o'er the wrecks of time." Wherever Christianity goes, it is best known by the cross.

Easter also transformed a tomb, which was the most awesome symbol of our mortality, weakness, and death. It was the prison from which no person could ever go free. There were other prisons from which men and women could escape, but no person could ever go free of the tomb. It was there that men and women fought their last great battle and always lost. It was there that death was king and reigned with undisputed power.

Some women made their way just at the breaking of day to the tomb of Jesus, only to discover that it was empty. A messenger, whom they did not know, announced: "He has risen, he is not here." And then with a gesture of the hand, he continued: "See the place where they laid him."

The tomb was transformed in the light of that morning. The tomb was no longer the undisputed domain of death. The tomb was under a new authority, under the power of the living, reigning Lord of life. When the early Christians looked back upon that tomb, it was a symbol of God's mighty power over death. Paul spoke of the immeasurable greatness of God's power "which he accomplished in Christ when he raised him from the dead" (Eph. 1:20).

Easter transformed the cross and the tomb. What transformations they are!

Time

Easter's transformation was not only felt in the world of things but in the world of time as well. It transformed two days in particular: Friday, the day of Jesus' death, and Sunday, the day of His resurrection.

If we had been at the scene of Jesus' crucifixion we would not have called it a good day. The effects of blind prejudice, arrogant pride, aborted justice, and sins of the human heart were darker than the blackest midnight. The one man with pure, unmuddled motives that earth had known was put to death on a felon's cross. It was a day when evil seemed to have won a complete victory. It was a day with deep and foreboding shadows lying across it, shadows later absorbed in darkness. Nature seemed to be shocked at what it saw, for darkness lay upon the earth from noon until three o'clock. What was good about that day? It seemed to be a day lying totally in the grip of evil. Yet, we call it Good Friday.

What made the difference? Easter. The light of Easter morning fell across that day, scattering its shadows and driving away its darkness. In that light, the day looked so different. God was there, indeed there in a way He had never been in any other day. He was judging the evil of men and absorbing in His great love the sins of men, even the sins that nailed His dear Son to the cross. That terrible Friday was God's day when He was breaking the back of evil, healing the wounds it had inflicted, and overcoming the estrangement it had caused. The worst day of history became the best day. Indeed, it is Good Friday.

Another day was transformed. It was the first day of the week when Jesus was resurrected. It had been a secular day, but within a generation of the resurrection of Jesus, it became a day of worship for Christians, the most sacred day of the week. Sunday replaced the Jewish sabbath.

This was radical action for Christians. In creating their own day of worship, Christians were breaking from their parent religion at a very crucial point. The sabbath was such a powerful day. It was the

Jewish day of rest and worship. They worshiped God the Creator on the sabbath. Because God had rested the seventh day of creation, they rested that day. A sacred hush fell over the sabbath, and with the centuries the day had grown in veneration and sacredness. The Fourth Commandment protected it: "Remember the sabbath day, to keep it holy" (Ex. 20:8). In order to keep its holiness and sacredness inviolate, the Jews had fenced it in and guarded it with innumerable laws. No day was so carefully protected and deeply revered.

The break with the sabbath must have been painful indeed. But the resurrection of Jesus was so powerful that Christians chose the day of resurrection as their day of worship. After a hard day of work, the Christians would gather in a home to worship God who did a new creation in Christ; there they worshiped in the name of their resurrected Lord. They met in certain assurance that their living Lord was in their midst. The sacred hush that had fallen over the sabbath for centuries would now fall over the Day of Resurrection, the first day of the week.

Message

We live not only in a world of things and time but also a world of ideas and faith. Easter made its impact here.

It would be wrong to believe that the early Christians totally rejected the Jewish message. They did not. But that message was fulfilled and transformed by the coming of Jesus. The old message was made new.

If it had not been for Easter, we would have no distinctively Christian message for our world. Without the resurrection, Jesus of Nazareth would be just another of those many tragic and pitiable figures destroyed by the evil forces of our world. He could hold out no hope for the world. Paul believed that without the resurrection the structure of Christian faith would fall apart, and our gospel would be null and void. He said, "If Christ has not been raised, then our preaching is in vain and your faith is in vain. . . . If Christ has not been raised, your faith is futile and you are still in your sins" (1 Cor. 15:14,17).

We feel the blows of despair that come in rapid succession upon us if Christ has not been raised; preaching is vain, faith is futile, and we are still in our sins. Paul was saying that we really have no message without the resurrection; faith is empty, and we cannot expect forgiveness of sins. How could a dead savior ever forgive sins?

It was Easter that made possible the greatest message our world has ever heard.

Men and women have never gone forth more boldly and with greater confidence than did those early Christians. They went saying that God had acted mightily on behalf of people everywhere in Jesus Christ: He did it out of a great love for His world. Men and women found the answer to their sins in the death of Jesus, and they found the answer to their deaths in the resurrection of Jesus. There was hope for people bent beneath their heavy burdens of guilt, and there was hope for men and women walking through the shadows into the night of their deaths.

At first, the message was transmitted orally. Eyewitnesses, people who had known Jesus and heard Him, shared the good news. But with the passing of the first generation of Christians, they knew the message needed something more permanent than oral transmission. So our Gospels were written by men who had known Jesus or by ones who were intimate with those who had known Him. Paul and others wrote letters that became a part of our New Testament. But it was the resurrection that made the message worth telling and worth writing.

This message, validated by the resurrection, is just as fresh, relevant, and powerful as when it was first preached and written. Men and women still exult in the forgiveness of sins and in the assurance of life everlasting. And we can face anything if we have the living Christ to go with us. We cling to the promise He has made us: "Lo, I am with you always, to the close of the age" (Matt. 28:20). He will keep His promise.

William Barclay, in his book *A Spiritual Autobiography,* tells about his twenty-one-year-old daughter and the young man she would have married being drowned in a yachting accident. The tragedy, of course, was numbing and heartbreaking. Barclay said it was no use asking *why*. Mystery hangs over an experience like that. We cannot understand, and it is harmful and destructive to become bitter and cynical. But there is something better than knowing and certainly something better than bitterness and cynicism: go on living, go on working, and find in the presence of the living Christ the strength and courage we need to face life. We can do that if we believe in the resurrection and know the Person of Easter.

Human Life

We would be surprised if Easter changed things and time and left human life untouched. But we are not surprised: men and women are changed by the power of Easter. These changed people are a part of the Easter story.

Whereas the disciples of Jesus once dreamed of power, glory, and victory, Easter morning found them withdrawn from the world, locked behind closed doors. They were weak, frightened, and disillusioned men. All strength and hope had left them. Then the risen Lord appeared in their midst.

Under the impact of Easter, something happened to these men. Their weakness gave way to strength, their doubt to faith, their despair to hope, their cowardice to courage, and their narrow nationalistic vision to a vision for the whole world.

They were now eager and ready. Yet they were not to rush out in their own strength. Jesus felt He needed to restrain them: "You are witnesses of these things," Jesus told them. "Behold, I send the promise of my father upon you; but stay in the city, until you are clothed with power from on high" (Luke 24:48-49).

We could find no better example of an Easter transformation than the apostle Paul. He met the resurrected Lord along a dusty road on the way to Damascus. He hated Christians with a passion and was on his way to help do away with the new movement. He had been intensely devout in his religious practice. He had studied, prayed, and lived his faith in great devotion. He was brilliant, gifted, and intense. Yet upon meeting the risen Christ, Paul's future as he envisioned it was shattered. Never has a person done a more radical about-face. Paul called Lord Him whom he had hated and became a member of the fellowship he had sworn to destroy. Rather than continuing as a persecutor, Paul was willing to become one of the persecuted. He hated that which he once loved and loved that which he had once hated. No wonder Paul could speak of being a new creation in Christ. His life had been transformed!

The Easter message was taken into a world where human life was cheap. A high percentage of the population were slaves. Women were little more than chattels, and often children were not wanted, especially baby girls.

Christianity gave a new value and dignity to people. Those who thought of themselves as being worthless were told that through Christ they could become the children of God. Nobodies became *somebodies*. Peter could say: "Once you were no people but now you are God's people; once you had not received mercy but now you have received mercy" (1 Pet. 2:10). Authentic Christianity has always been, and still is, the most elevating influence in all of history.

Death

We live in a world of death. Nature dies, men and women die, and the things we create with our hands and minds at last perish. There is a terrible grimness about life. We must all die.

The meaning of death was transformed by Easter. Those who stood in the early morning of the resurrection saw that death was not the end. Death brought its tears and grief, but there was no longer a sense of defeat. They experienced a sense of victory and triumph.

Do you feel the sense of triumph in the Scripture lesson? It was as if the funeral dirge had given way to a shout of victory: "O death, where is thy sting? O grave, where is thy victory?" (1 Cor. 15:55, KJV).

Easter makes us want to shout.

William E. Songster, the gifted British Methodist preacher, suffered from muscular atrophy. For two years he endured suffering with unlimited courage. One Easter day, in the grip of the disease, unable to walk or speak, he wrote his daughter. "It is terrible to wake up on Easter morning and have no voice with which to shout, He is risen—but it would be still more terrible to have a voice and not want to shout."

At the close of the Passion Play at Oberammergau, Germany, after the resurrection and glorification of Jesus, the chorus sings: "Hallelujah! Praise, renown, adoration, power and glory be Thine for ever and ever."

Death is not the end. There is something beyond. Easter tells us so.

For centuries, Western Europe believed the world ended at the Pillars of Hercules—two promontories at the eastern end of the Strait of Gibraltar. There was a time when Spain stamped on her coins the pillars of Hercules and underneath the Latin words *ne plus ultra* which meant "no more beyond." Then Columbus sailed through those pillars to discover the New World. Spain still carried on her coins the pillars of Hercules but changed the inscription to read *plus ultra* which means "more beyond." The resurrection did something like that to death. There is much more beyond.

Thus the resurrection gave to life a meaning that lay beyond death. It gave life an ultimate meaning. It set life within eternal dimensions.

John Knox tells of visiting a church in eastern Virginia where his father had been pastor some fifty years earlier. Knox said his father was quiet and modest, a man of remarkable intelligence, charm, and quite extraordinary goodness. Some of the oldest members remembered him vividly, but they were few, and would become fewer each year until they were all gone. Then there would be no one to remember father. His name would be remembered, for there was a memorial bearing his name. But that name would mean little or nothing to the new generation. "Here is perhaps the supreme pathos of human life," Knox wrote, "not that we die only but that any real and living memory must die, too. Unless God is to raise us from death it is the end as though we had never lived."

Easter assures us that God raised Jesus from the dead, and He will raise us.

Easter transformations! How wonderful they are. We are asked to be open to the living, resurrected Christ so that Easter may again work its transformation in us.

10
Easter's Invitation and Imperative

(Matt. 28:1-10)

The Christian life alternates between invitation and imperative. This is not seen anywhere more clearly than in the Easter story.

The women visiting the tomb of Jesus early in the morning met an angel of the Lord who sat on the stone that had been rolled away from the entrance. He quieted their fears in the firm assurance that Jesus was risen. He gave them as invitation: "Come, see the place where he lay." Then the angel sent them forth under an urgent imperative: "Go quickly and tell his disciples that he has risen from the dead."

The church, therefore, when it is true to its Easter faith moves, like a pendulum, between invitation and imperative.

Invitation

The Easter invitation is true to the spirit of the Bible that constantly addresses our deepest needs. Listen to several invitations of grace. "Ho, every one who thirsts, / come to the waters: / and he who has no money, / come, buy and eat! / Come, buy wine and milk / without money and without price" (Isa. 55:1). "Come to me, all who labor and are heavy laden, and I will give you rest" (Matt. 11:28). At the end of our Scriptures, another invitation of grace is given. "The Spirit and the Bride say, 'Come.' And let him who hears say, 'Come.' And let him who is thirsty come, let him who desires take the water of life without price" (Rev. 22:17).

These invitations obviously are not ours to make. We are invited to see something we have not done, hear something we have not spoken, and accept something we could not give. We are invited to eat at banquets we did not prepare and drink from fountains we did not prime. We are invited to receive forgiveness we could not offer, healing we could not give, and life we who are caught in the grip of death could never offer. We are invited to see an empty tomb whose victim we could not have brought forth from the dead.

We are invited not only to come but to see. Here we feel the New Testament's great emphasis on personal experience, on the first-handedness of faith. We are invited to see, feel, handle, and experience. There is an indispensable relationship between seeing and witnessing, one of the great themes of the New Testament. Jesus said to His disciples after His resurrection: "You shall be my witnesses" (Acts 1:8). A witness is one who knows firsthand. He tells what he has seen, heard, and experienced. He does not tell what others have said and heard. He does not theorize and speculate. He tells what he knows.

Authentic witnessing is powerful. It is moving to hear a person say: "I was being destroyed by guilt, and Christ forgave me," or, "My life was like a raging sea, and Christ gave me peace," or, "My life was being burned up by hatred, and Christ enabled me to love." You cannot refute that kind of reality.

The most important person in the early church was the apostle, and the primary qualification for being an apostle was to have seen Jesus. Paul, who, so far as we know, never saw the historic Jesus, claimed to be an apostle because belatedly he had seen the resurrected Christ along the Damascus road. "Last of all," he wrote, "as one untimely born, he appeared also to me" (1 Cor. 15:8).

No visitor excited the early church like an apostle. Little groups of worshiping Christians, sometimes far removed from the land where Jesus was born and lived, were thrilled to meet and hear someone who had known Jesus. Second only to hearing an apostle was receiving a letter written by one. Imagine a leader announcing to the little congregation at Corinth: "I understand a letter from the apostle Paul is on its way and should be here on the next Lord's Day. I will read it to you then." They could hardly wait for the week to pass. They wanted a word from a man who had seen and known Jesus Christ.

When it came time for the church to select the books that would officially make up the New Testament, the one thing that gave a book its greatest eligibility was to have been written by an apostle, one who had seen the Lord.

It is just as important that the same kind of thing happen in the modern church. Our Bible was born of encounters between God and people and between people and people. We must relive the experiences of the Bible, set within our time, and have the kinds of encounters out of which our Bible came. We must be able to say: "I have seen, I have felt, I have known."

The theology of the modern church, when it is great theology, is born of living experience. Theology should be the critical reflection of that experience, and the crucial question of theology is not how logical and rational it is, but is it able to recapture the experience on which it has been reflecting?

On Easter we can't be invited to see the empty tomb of our Lord. It no longer exists. But we are invited to see evidence of the risen Lord just as convincing as His empty tomb. And beyond that, there are possibilities of fresh encounters with the risen and living Christ.

Elizabeth Achtemeier tells of a clergy friend of hers who was terminally ill with cancer. He wrote her shortly before his death: "You ask for my insights on preaching. I guess the one thing that I see as I look over a ministry from which I am now some distance removed is the importance of preaching what one has experienced. Otherwise it's hearsay."[1]

Imperative

The invitation of Easter quickly passed into imperative: "Go quickly and tell his disciples that he has risen from the dead" (Matt. 28:7).

The women were sent on a mission, and they felt urgently about it. "So they departed quickly from the tomb with fear and great joy, and ran to tell his disciples." They did not wait and loiter around. No time was wasted. They were immediately on their way.

The church can never really encounter Easter and not have its life set under an imperative. It is sent on a mission. Easter gives feet to the church and shoves it on mission. The church must always be a pilgrim, a traveler. It must be going places. At times it will not go far, at other times it must go to the far ends of the earth.

One of the weirdest characters of the New Testament is the Gadarene demoniac (Mark 5, KJV; Luke 8). He lived among the tombs and his wild shrieks at night often awoke the villagers. Many people went forth in the early morning to the duties of the day not having slept the previous night. The wild man of the tombs had kept them awake. He cut himself with stones and he was exceedingly strong. They bound him with fetters and chains, and like Houdini, he went free of them. The people of the village didn't know how to cope with him. Then Jesus healed him, making him well and whole. As Jesus made ready to leave, the healed man followed Him to His boat and pleaded with Him for the privilege of going with Him. But why the request?

Maybe the Gadarene was caught up in the romance of travel with its new places that would seem strange and far away since he probably had never left his village. Did he dream of the big towns on the other side of the lake, the rich fields of barley and wheat, and long caravans of commerce moving north and south? Or did he just want to be with the man who had had mercy on him and healed him? In any case, Jesus would not grant his request. "Go home to your friends," Jesus said, "and tell them how much the Lord has done for you, and how he has had mercy on you."

The Gadarene was to go as a witness, as one who told what the Lord had done for him. He was not to go far away—back to the village, his family, and his friends.

The church is under an imperative that sometimes does not send it far away. It lives its life and bears its witness in a village or town. If it doesn't bear its witness well there, it will not bear it well anywhere. Credibility is either made or lost where the church lives.

But the church is under an imperative that sends it far away, to the ends of the earth. "Go into all the world," said Jesus, "and preach the gospel to the whole creation" (Mark 16:15).

The women were not only to go, they were to tell: "Tell his disciples that he has risen from the dead, and behold, he is going before you to Galilee" (Matt. 28:7).

It was not worthwhile to go unless they had something to tell. As they stood beside the empty tomb of Jesus, the women experienced the most exciting news the world has ever had: Jesus Christ has risen from the dead! As they looked into that empty tomb, they were seeing that which was unique, unrepeatable, and final. What good news they had to share!

The question Easter answered basically was not: Will the truth of Jesus continue? Nor, will His influence live on? The question was: Will Jesus, who claimed to give life, live on? Will He survive death?

Socrates was one of the wisest and best men history has known. He was a lover of and a teacher of truth. Yet he got into trouble with the power structure of Athens and it put him to death. His followers saw him drink the hemlock and die peacefully. They were able to say: "Athens could kill Socrates, but they could not stop his influence or destroy his truth." But Easter made a much bolder claim: "Jerusalem and Rome not only failed to destroy Jesus' truth, they could not destroy Him. He has gone free of His tomb."

Tom Skinner has asked: "How do you stop Jesus? How do you stop a man who has no guns, no tanks, no ammunition, but still is shaking the Roman Empire. How do you stop a man—who without firing a gun is getting revolutionary results?" The answer is: "We can't stop Him. He has conquered the last and most formidable enemy, death itself. He is now unconquerable."

Those women could go boldly and confidently. In a sense, the resurrection is the most crucial event in Christian faith. It is the keystone that holds the arch together. Without it the arch collapses; with it, the structure holds.

How do we tell the good news? This is done essentially two ways—by deed and by word.

We should have a life-style, a manner of living, that announces the good news of our faith. We should be those who live in the light of Easter morning, not in the shadows of darkness and despair. We should never forget it was love that sent Jesus to His cross and brought Him forth from the tomb on Easter morning. That same love should motivate and control us.

An extremely bright, young Oriental woman was awarded a scholarship to study on the campus of a Christian college in the

South. She was not a Christian, and there was considerable discussion among the students as to who could best convince her of the merit of Christianity. Eventually, she became a Christian, but she was not won by the brilliant arguments of a gifted student. Instead, she told of an almost completely unknown coed: "She didn't use arguments," the new convert said, "She built a bridge from her heart to mine, so Christ walked over it."

Yet, verbal witness, when sincerely given from a committed life, is very powerful, and we are under obligation to give it. God will hold us responsible for witnessing to the risen Christ and His power to save.

Martin Niemöller, one of Hitler's famous prisoners, told of a dream that impressed him with his responsibility for witnessing to others. He said he had felt no obligation to witness to his Nazi guards until he had a dream during the seventh year of his eight-year imprisonment. In his dream, he saw Hitler pleading his case before the judgment bar of God. His excuse for his sins was that he never heard the gospel. Then Niemöller heard God ask, "Were you not with him a whole hour without telling him the gospel?" Awakening, he remembered that he had been alone with Hitler for a whole hour without witnessing to him. What if he had told Hitler about the risen Christ who is able to forgive sins and redeem lives? What a difference it might have made.

The church is under a strong imperative to go and tell. It must be indefatigable in its effort. It has a word to speak without which the world will die in its sins.

The late Arnold T. Ohrn once told of a Christian in India who had been beaten and driven from his home by fellow villagers. But he came back. A friend met him at the gate of the village and asked: "Why would you return to the village? Don't you know they will flog you again, sending you away from your home?" To this the man replied: "Did you hear about the conclave of the animals?" The he proceeded to tell this story:

There was a great drought in the forest. They had had no rain for a long time. Springs failed, the streams were drying up, vegetation was withering and dying, and the animals seemed to be facing certain starvation and death. So a conclave was called. The leading animals of the forest were there and so were the smaller animals. Mr. Giraffe, the tallest, presided. He stated the purpose of the conclave. The springs were failing, the streams were drying up, vegetation was dying, and their little ones panted themselves to sleep at night. Death seemed to be coming upon them. The question was: What can we do to survive? The most powerful and influential animals had the floor but they were floundering, and they seemed to be going in a circle. On the outskirts of the assembly was a turtle who with his squeaky voice had been trying to say something but had been completely ignored. When the discussion had about finished, Mr. Giraffe finally recognized the turtle: "What are you trying to say, Mr. Turtle?" Mr. Turtle replied, "I know where there is water."

The Christian then said to his friend: "I go back to the village, not because I am smarter or better than they are. But my fellow villagers are thirsty, and I know where there is water."

We live in a world where many people are dying of thirst. The springs of hope have failed, and the streams of expectation have dried up. The church knows where there is water. The church has an evangelistic and missionary task it dare not fail to fulfill.

D. T. Miles once said that evangelism is one beggar telling another beggar where there is bread. It is one thirsty person telling another thirsty person where there is water, one sick person telling another sick person where there is healing, and one sinner telling another sinner where there is forgiveness. It is one person knowing that he or she must die all too soon, telling another caught in the same fate that there is an empty tomb, where life can be had.

The invitation on Easter is as fresh as when morning first broke over that empty tomb. We are invited to come to Him who, having conquered death, is now the Giver of life. But He will not let us tarry too long. With a strong hand, He shoves us back into the world where we are to share the life He has given. It is still invitation and imperative.

Note

1. Elizabeth Actemeier, quoted in *The Minister's Manual*, 1974 ed. (n.p., 1974), 34-35.

11
A Trilogy
of Powerful Events

(Acts 1:1-11; 2:1-4)

Christianity is a religion of events, not abstract ideas. It is too alive and down to earth to be lost in abstractions. Things happen in our faith. There are meetings and encounters, goings forth and returnings, judgments and forgiveness, woundings and healings of mercy.

In our Scripture lesson we encounter three powerful events: the resurrection, the ascension, and the gift of the Spirit. They are very important. Take away the resurrection, and Christianity is destroyed. Dent the ascension and the gift of the Spirit, and that would greatly impair our faith. It would go limping without power.

These events tell us something essential about God in His relation to us and our world. God is behind us in the historic and resurrected Lord. He is above us in the ascended and cosmic Christ. He is with us, beside us, in the Holy Spirit. God sustains a historic, transcendent, and immanent relationship with us. Here is found one of the secrets of the greatness of Christianity.

Resurrection

The story of the resurrection is not told in our Scripture lesson, but we cannot escape its reality. We meet the resurrected Lord who will not let us forget the resurrection. He is living proof that it has occurred.

Jesus stayed with His disciples for forty days. It is interesting that Luke tells us the exact time He was with them. Forty was an important number in Jewish history and faith. Moses stayed forty days on Mount Sinai. The children of Israel wandered for forty years in the wilderness. Jesus fasted for forty days in the wilderness before He was tempted by the devil. The mention of that number would not let them forget that Jesus was a part of Israel's long and dramatic history.

We see how quickly the Easter story shifts from the empty tomb to the risen Lord. Nothing further is said about it. They didn't need to mention it as the risen Lord was in their midst.

Here is an interesting thing: there is not a sharp break in the continuity of the earthly life of Jesus and His resurrected life. He is without doubt the same Person; He talked the way He did before His crucifixion, and He was concerned about the same great themes. He did not talk in a strange speech. And He did not introduce esoteric ideas. In the postresurrection meeting with Peter along the Sea of Galilee, Jesus talked about love which had been the great ethical passion of his life. He wanted to make sure that Peter loved above all else.

Luke tells us that during the forty days Jesus was with them He talked about the kingdom of God. That is what He had talked with them about before His resurrection. The kingdom of God is the overarching theme of the New Testament. Mark introduces Jesus' great Galilean ministry like this: "Jesus came into Galilee, preaching the gospel of God, and saying, 'The time is fulfilled, and the kingdom of God is at hand; repent, and believe in the gospel'" (1:14-15).

What an hour! It was as if God were knocking on their doors, announcing His reign. Their old order was being invaded by God's order.

God's kingdom! How strange it was. They didn't understand it. They tried to fit it into their old ideas and structures. They politicized it. Images of power and grandeur danced in their minds. They envisioned marching and victorious armies. Their nation would be restored to its former glory. Jesus tried to help them understand that His kingdom would be different, but to the very end they clung to their old ideas. They asked him: "Lord, will you at this time restore the kingdom of Israel?" (v. 6). It was not the kingdom of God they wanted restored but the kingdom of Israel. They didn't dream of a kingdom embracing all people, with all geographical, cultural, national, racial, and religious barriers transcended.

It was for the kingdom of God that Jesus had taught His disciples to pray: "Our Father who art in heaven, / Hallowed be thy name, / Thy kingdom come, / Thy will be done, / On earth as it is in heaven" (Matt. 6:9-10).

The prayer explains what the kingdom of God is to be: "Thy will be done, / On earth as it is in heaven." The kingdom of God comes when the will of God is done on earth, not only in religion but also in the social, political, and economic areas. It will not come with marching armies, the clashing of swords, warfare in space, and the spilling of blood. While it is to be worked for and striven after, it will come at last as a gift—the gift of God's love and justice.

Ascension

The ascension follows the resurrection.

The disciples went with Jesus to the Mount of Olives. Luke tells us that "as they were looking on, he was lifted up, and a cloud took him out of their sight" (Acts 1:9).

It is a good time to note a basic movement in biblical faith: up and down, ascent and descent.

Jacob's ladder can be a symbol of that movement. Jacob was fleeing from Esau, his brother, and night overtook him. He slept beneath the stars on the ground with a stone as a pillow beneath his head. It was a barren spot with nothing to remind him of God. Yet, it became a holy place before the night was over. Jacob dreamed "that there was a ladder set up on the earth, and the top of it reached to heaven; and behold, the angels of God were ascending and descending on it!" (Gen. 28:12). There was the upward and downward movement, ascent and descent. This movement continues throughout the Bible: movement between earth and heaven, the seen and the unseen, time and eternity, history and beyond history, the natural and the supernatural.

This movement is seen in the ascension. Jesus Christ, the Son of God, had come down from God. Now He was going back. Ascension was a part of that upward, spiraling movement.

Ascension has at least three important meanings: it points to a place of honor, speaks of relational reality, and tells about something of cosmic significance.

First, ascension is concerned with a position of honor.

The New Testament speaks of Jesus as being seated at the right hand of God. Paul writes: "If then you have been raised with Christ, seek the things that are above, where Christ is, seated at the right hand of God" (Col. 3:1).

If you were having guests tonight and one of them were particularly distinguished, worthy of special honor, where would you seat him? To the right of the hostess, which is the seat of honor. Christ is seated at the right hand of God in the place of honor.

He is the same person who was humiliated, beaten, and spat upon. He is the one who wore the purple robe, who had the crown of thorns pressed upon His head, and who died the shameful death of a Roman cross. It is all so different now. He occupies a position next to God, the most prestigious place in the universe.

Further, the ascension points to a relational reality rather than spacial.

It is easy to hold to an ancient cosmology that has earth at the center with heaven above and hell beneath. With that view of the world, it is easy to see God sitting on a throne above the earth with Christ at His right hand. If that were the case, the ascension would speak of spacial reality. But this is not the case.

When the first Russian cosmonaut went into space and returned, he remarked that he did not see God up there anywhere. Of course he did not. He was looking for God in the wrong place.

Finally, the ascension has a cosmic significance. When I speak of cosmic, I mean that which is above earth with its history, beyond the space-time dimension.

We speak of Christianity as being a historical religion, and it is important that we do. We remember again that God has revealed Himself in history, that He made His ultimate revelation in a historical person: Jesus of Nazareth. But the historical can never exhaust the full meaning of Christian faith. Christianity has a cosmic dimension.

Christ has been cosmic from the beginning. John pictures Christ as being with God before creation. He was the agent of creation: "All things were made through him and without him was not anything made that was made" (John 1:3). Paul says that "in him all things were created, in heaven and on earth, visible and invisible, whether thrones or dominions or principalities or authorities—all things were created through him and for him" (Col. 1:16).

Sin and evil are cosmic. Separation and alienation are cosmic. Not only has rebellion taken place on earth, it has occurred beyond earth. The break that lies across the human heart and human history extends out into the universe. History is rifted and so is the universe. In a sense, riftness is the great reality of our existence, historic and cosmic. We need to be healed.

Paul talked of the mystery that God had kept until the coming of Jesus. Paul spoke about that mystery "as a plan for the fulness of time, to unite all things in him, things in heaven and on earth" (Eph. 1:10). Jesus' mission was not only to unite separated people on earth but to reconcile rebellious and warring powers beyond earth. Reconciliation is cosmic, salvation is cosmic. It is such a big, sweeping concept. I can't imagine anything more exciting.

From His cosmic position of power, Jesus will return some day to consummate history. As the disciples saw Jesus being taken away from them, two men in white robes said to them: "Men of Galilee, why do you stand looking into heaven? This Jesus, who was taken up from you into heaven, will come in the same way as you saw him go into heaven" (Acts 1:11).

The Gift of the Spirit

We could probably sustain the claim that the coming of the Holy Spirit is the fourth most important event in the Christian religion, superceded only by the birth, death, and resurrection of Jesus.

The Holy Spirit was given on the Day of Pentecost. The term *Pentecost* means "the fiftieth." It is the Greek name for the Hebrew Feast of Weeks that commemorated the giving of the Law. Pentecost occurred fifty days after Passover.

There were three great Jewish festivals that every male Jew, living within twenty miles of Jerusalem, was legally bound to attend: Passover, Pentecost, and Feast of Tabernacles. Pentecost fell at the beginning of June when traveling conditions were at their best. Therefore, probably larger crowds attended Pentecost than even Passover.

Great crowds were in Jerusalem for Pentecost when the Holy Spirit came upon the people. The story says, "There were dwelling in Jerusalem Jews, devout men from every nation under heaven" (Acts 2:5).

There are two things that make that Pentecost especially important. First, the gift of the Holy Spirit came upon the people like "the rush of a mighty wind" from heaven. The imagery of power is unmistakable. Second, the first and most powerful sermon in the history of the Christian church was preached that day, and fortunately, we have an account of that sermon.

What happened at Pentecost does not mean that God's Spirit had not been present in the world. God has always been present in His creation in His Spirit.

The psalmist asked, "Whither shall I go from thy Spirit? / Or whither shall I flee from thy presence?" (Ps. 139:7). He concluded that there was no way to escape God's Spirit. If he ascended into heaven, if he descended into Sheol, if he dwelt in the uttermost parts of the sea, he would find God. There was no nook or corner in the universe where God was not.

What then made the coming of the Spirit at Pentecost unique? Four things: first, while the gift of the Spirit in Israel's life had been restricted to a select few, her leaders and prophets, at Pentecost it was poured out upon all believers. Luke sees Pentecost as a fulfillment of Joel's prophecy that said in part: "In the last days it shall be, God declares, / that I will pour out my Spirit upon all flesh" (Acts 2:17). Not only would prophets, seers, and wise men be given the Spirit, but the simplest people—maids, cooks, butlers, slaves, and others—would receive it, too.

Second, the Holy Spirit would be like Jesus. He would think, act, and behave like Jesus. Because of this, the Spirit in the New Testament would have a clearer image than the Spirit in the Old Testament. He is like Jesus.

In the early experience of the church it was hard to distinguish between Jesus and the Spirit. Paul could write:

> Now the Lord is the Spirit, and where the Spirit of the Lord is, there is freedom. And we all, with unveiled face, beholding the glory of the

Lord, are being changed into his likeness from one degree of glory to another; for this comes from the Lord who is the Spirit (2 Cor. 3:17-18).

In Acts, it was the Spirit who took the place of Jesus. The Spirit guided, illumined, directed, and empowered. Some have said that the Acts of the Apostles should be the Acts of the Spirit or the Gospel of the Holy Spirit.

Third, the Holy Spirit would empower preaching.

I have already spoken of Peter's sermon on Pentecost as being the greatest sermon ever preached. How could that be? Peter was really not a preacher. He was not an eloquent and highly gifted man. If you had put a book of homiletics in Peter's hand, he would not have known what he was holding. What was the secret of his power and greatness? The Holy Spirit more than anything else.

We still need the Holy Spirit in our pulpits. How often our sermons are well formed and well balanced, having perfect homiletical structure. Yet they do not live. They do not have power. They are like those bodies Ezekiel saw on the desert sand. They had perfect form, but they did not live. It was only after God breathed His Spirit into them that they stood to their feet a mighty, living host. It is only as God breathes His Spirit into our homiletical forms that our sermons will have power.

Fourth, the Holy Spirit took a diverse group of people with widely differing geographical and cultural backgrounds and united them. They were all amazed, for as these Galileans preached, the people heard them in their own language. It is little wonder they were perplexed, asking, "What does this mean?"

It was as if Babel was reversed at Pentecost. Do you remember how God brought judgment upon men living in the land of Shinar? They were exceedingly ambitious and wanted to usurp God's power. So they began to build a tower that would reach into heaven. The people were unified, but God broke their unity by giving them different languages. The place where this happened was Babel (Babylon). The barrier of language is a high and formidable one. The language barrier that was cast up at Babel was broken down at Pentecost. Mystery hangs over Pentecost. We don't completely understand what took place. But one thing is clear: The language barrier, however it happened, was broken down, and people from diverse backgrounds were unified.

Next to Jesus Christ Himself, the Holy Spirit is the most prominent reality in the life of the early church. The members of that church came from everywhere, representing many languages, cultures, nationalities, races, and religions. Yet they found a oneness in Christ and His church. The Holy Spirit played such an important role in this that Paul could write: "For just as the body is one and has many members, and all the members of the body, though many, are one body, so it is with Christ. For by one Spirit we were all baptized into one body—Jews or Greeks, slaves or free—and all were made to drink of one Spirit" (1 Cor. 12:12-13).

The barriers—racial, cultural, and socioeconomic—are often still standing in the church. Some of our churches do not want people of other races. The social stratification of our society is clearly seen in our churches. We take secular standards of success, cover them with a thin religious veneer, and adopt them as our own. Often we prefer socially congenial people to spiritually sensitive persons in our church fellowship. Frequently, we are more like a club choosing those we want and rejecting those we do not want. We seem to forget that it is not we but Christ who chooses those who will belong to His church. How badly we need the Spirit to break down these barriers and unite us around Christ in love, affirmation, and ministry.

Our prayer should be: "Come, Holy Spirit! Let Pentecost happen again."

12
The Risen Lord
Speaks of Love

(John 21:1-17)

Jesus believed that the most powerful force, not only in history but in the universe, is love. Unlike other forms of power that strut and parade in an effort to hide their weaknesses, love—knowing itself to be strong—dares to appear weak, as on Good Friday. Jesus looked so weak stumbling beneath His cross through the streets of jeering people. Yet on that day with its parade of power, Jesus alone was strong.

Jesus, reflecting the moral reality of life, gave a new commandment, "that you love one another; even as I have loved you, that you also love one another" (John 13:34). He told His disciples that the world would recognize them as His followers only as they lived by this commandment.

Jesus Christ, having crossed the great abyss of death and returned, still talked of love. One of the most beautiful stories in the New Testament is told in the twenty-first chapter of John. After the resurrection in the early dawn Jesus appeared as a stranger to seven of His disciples who had fished all night long on the Sea of Galilee without making a single catch. He was soon recognized as the risen Lord. After breakfast, Jesus and Simon Peter walked along a seashore that carried so many memories. Jesus asked Simon Peter three times: "Simon, son of John, do you love me more than these?" (v. 15). Jesus could have asked Peter many questions, but He wanted to know upon whom Peter's heart was set supremely. Jesus knew that nothing could ever be right in Peter's life until his heart was right.

Jesus comes to us with his postresurrection question: "Do you love Me more than these?"

Sentimental Things

Peter had been in and out of Capernaum for the last year or so, but he was home again that morning. He was among familiar places and familiar faces. He had grown up along that seashore. He remembered as a little boy how he and his friends had made castles of sand with their hands, only to have the waves come lapping in and wash them away forever. He had learned to swim in those waters; he had sailed his first boat on them. As a young man Peter had gone into business along that shore. Just down the road were Mrs. Simon Peter and the children. He had planned to go home soon for breakfast and tell the news of a night's labor lost.

There was no sand so white and shimmering as the sand along that shore, no sky so pure by day and brilliant by night as the sky above that place, no water so blue as the water of that sea. How Peter loved that place! He was bound to it by a thousand sentimental ties. Then he heard Jesus asking him: "Simon, son of John, do you love me more than these [sentimental things of life]?"

Sentiment is a soft way of thinking about things, persons and life. It has its place, but it can get in the way of an effective Christian life.

I have known many people who thought sentimentally about their church. They remembered nostalgically the church of their childhood. They would say the loveliest things about the church, yet they were never willing to undergo the discipline of churchmanship. They let others give the leadership, do the work, and pay the bills.

I remember a man who was richly endowed with gifts and personality. I used to talk with him about uniting with our church, but he would not hear me. He would tell me about the church in the eastern part of the state where he grew up. His mother and father were buried there. Moreover, it was weak and struggling, and what money he had he must share with that church. The years passed, and on the day of his funeral I could not help thinking that he had contributed nothing to our church and little, if anything, to the church of his early years. What was the problem? Certainly in part it was sentimentality. He gave devotion to a church that existed more in idealized memory than in reality.

If we listen to Jesus through sentimental ears we hear Him talking about the birds of the air and the flowers of the field. But we never hear His rigorous demands of Christian discipleship: "If any man would come after me, let him deny himself and take up his cross and follow me" (Matt. 16:24).

Boats, Nets, and Fishing Tackle

Peter stood among the boats, nets, and fishing tackle. These were the instruments of his livelihood. There was no stigma attached to these; they were tools of decent and hard work. Jesus was asking: Do you love Me more than the boats, nets, and fishing tackle?

If you had asked Peter if he loved these things, he would probably have denied it. Yet he did. Like us, he loved the things he possessed.

I remember a boy who lived just down the street from us. He owned a sports car in which he took great pride. He was constantly washing, shining, and waxing it. It had a rich sheen that was almost like a mirror. He never told me he loved his car. He didn't have to. I knew he did.

I have seen a full-fledged community grow up to the northwest of us. When I came to Martinsville, it was field and forest. Then after World War II a man erected the first building, a furniture store, in that area. One day I asked him why he chose that location, and he explained that when he came back from the war he was looking for a place to go into business; he reasoned that one day Martinsville and Bassett would meet there. As he told me his story, his eyes became moist, and there was a quiver of emotion in his voice. He didn't have to tell me he loved his business. I knew he did.

We love things, and we should love them. When God looked out upon his creation so rich with fields, streams, forest, and minerals, he said it was very good. We know God loved His creation.

If we should love things, then what is the problem? We love them too much. We are to be the masters of things, but too often they master us. How often we give lip service in the worship of Almighty God while we pour out our devotion at the altar of mammon. Yet there are few tyrannies, if any, more destructive than the tyranny of things. They forge chains and shackle us.

I think of the people I have known who sold their honor and integrity, destroyed their families, and wrecked their lives in the mad pursuit of things. Having been successful, they piled high about them their wealth only to discover late—too late—that the wealth they had amassed could not buy what their hearts really wanted.

Status symbols are one of the marks of our culture. Many of us are driven compulsively by them. We work our fingers to the bone in getting them. We find status in big houses, expensive cars, boats, summer houses, winter retreats, exclusive clubs, and wealthy friends. We sacrifice depth for glamor.

It is little wonder the Bible warns us often about the treachery of things and the deceptiveness of riches. Probably the most radical thing Jesus ever said was about riches: "It is easier for a camel to go through the eye of a needle than for a rich man to enter the kingdom of God" (Matt. 19:23).

When the Frankish king Charlemagne died, they did not give him a conventional burial. Rather than shrouding him, they put his royal robes on him and set him on his throne with an open Bible in his lap, the forefinger of his right hand pointing to these words: "For what will it profit a man, if he gains the whole world and forfeits his life?" (Matt. 16:26).

Friends

Peter was among his friends—six of them. He had traveled with them, eaten with them, laughed with them, and wept with them. He cared for them, and they cared for him. Their lives were inextricably involved with each other.

Peter was a good friend. He was easy to be with. He was warm, open, and affirming. He was the kind of person you could share most anything with. If you made a confession to him, you knew he would not be judgmental. Rather than wounding you further, he would try to heal you.

Jesus was asking: "Peter, do you love Me more than you love your friends?" It was a hard question.

Some of the hardest things Jesus ever said were about social relations. For example, "He who loves father or mother more than me is not worthy of me; and he who loves son or daughter more than me is not worthy of me" (Matt. 10:37).

That sounds harsh, but maybe it is not as severe as it sounds.

What if Peter loved Jesus first and best? Would he love his friends less? No. He would love them better and in healthier and more creative ways than he otherwise could have. The priority he gave Jesus would heighten his relationship with his friends.

I remember the day I set up a question for my mother. I asked it expecting a certain answer. "Mamma," I asked, "whom do you love best?" Because I had asked it I felt sure she would say *me*, but she didn't. She told me she loved God best of all, than Daddy, Melton, Mildred, and me. Because she loved God best, did that mean that she would love me less? No. It meant she would love me in ways she never could have loved me if she had not put God first.

My mother knew how to love me. She never loved me possessively. She never tried to fulfill through me some frustrated ambition in her own life. She loved me for who I was and for what I could become. She never kept me tied to herself, and she was always ready to release me to independent ways as soon as I was able to walk in them. Therefore, I can say that I owe much of my emotional health to my mother's influence.

In loving Jesus first, I am able to love others properly, seeing worth and beauty in them I would not otherwise be able to see.

There is that scarred face. It has always been ugly to me. I have tried to dodge the man. I would cross the street to avoid meeting him. I did this, not because I was ashamed of him, but because I didn't know how to respond. I felt awkward and self-conscious in his presence. Then one day the light that shone in the eyes of Jesus fell on that scarred face, and for the first time I saw how lovely it was.

His Own Life

There were the sentimental things, the boat, nets, and fishing tackle, and his friends. Isn't that about all? Yes, almost all, but not quite. Jesus was also asking, Peter, do you love Me more than your own life?

Life was his dearest possession. Nothing matters so much as life.

Why the beauty of the sea without human eyes to behold it? Why the boats, the nets, and the fishing tackle without human hands to man them? Why friendship without friends to give and receive it? Why anything without life?

But if Peter loved Jesus best of all, would Peter love himself less? No. He would love himself in accepting and affirming ways he never could have otherwise done.

Jesus told us we are to love ourselves: "You shall love your neighbor as yourself" (Matt. 22:39). But alas we do not love ourselves as we should. Indeed, within strict human dimensions that may be our great tragedy.

There are too many of us who do not love ourselves; we hate ourselves. We see little or no value, beauty, or worth in ourselves. We feel guilty, useless, empty, and worthless.

I have done a lot of counseling. About fifteen years ago I came to the conclusion that I had not worked with an emotionally distraught person who didn't have a poor self-image. While the evidence seemed to bear out the conclusion, it didn't seem right. So I talked with a professional counselor who confirmed my observation. A poor self-image was always the problem or a contributing factor.

How can we love ourselves as we should? How can we find beauty, value, and worth in our lives? I am suggesting two things that can help more than anything else: Jesus Christ and His church.

An old man had fallen along a medieval wayside. His clothes were worn and soiled, his face bearded, and his hair disheveled. He was thin and emaciated. He looked like a bum. Two doctors, speaking the scientific language of the time, which was Latin, passed by where he was. One doctor said to the other, "Let us take this worthless creature and experiment with him." Whereupon, the old man opened his eyes, and speaking perfect Latin scarcely above a whisper he said, "How dare you call anyone worthless for whom Christ died?"

The church has the ability to be the most accepting and affirming fellowship in the world. Knowing how much they have mattered to Christ, people in the church can also know how much they should matter to each other. Everybody should be somebody in the church.

THE RISEN LORD SPEAKS OF LOVE

There should be no cheap and worthless people in the Christian fellowship.

I know of a church covenant that, attempting to be contemporaneous, reads in part: "We shall love, accept, affirm, and pray for each other. There shall be no cheap person in our midst."

How shall we answer this postresurrection question: "Do you love me more than these?" If we could answer it positively, many of us would be delivered from our grasping, loveless, self-centered, materialistic, and tortured ways of life. Chains would be struck, and we would be delivered from our bondage into freedom.

13
He Appeared First to Mary Magdalene

(Mark 16:9-10; John 20:11-18)

Mark in his Easter story tells us that Jesus "appeared first to Mary Magdalene, from whom he had cast out seven demons." We are surprised, even shocked. We would have expected Jesus to appear first of all to His disciples, but He didn't.

Mark makes the announcement, but it is John who tells the story, set in a garden near where Jesus had been crucified. Mary was weeping. She turned and saw Jesus standing near her, but, being blinded by her tears, she did not recognize Him. "Woman, why are you weeping?" He asked. "Whom do you seek?" (v. 15). And Mary, believing Him to be the gardener, responded: "Sir, if you have carried him away, tell me where you have laid him, and I will take him away." Jesus simply called her by name, and Mary responded movingly, "Rabboni!" which means teacher.

The beauty of this warm, face-to-face, and heart-to-heart meeting lingers on. The years, rather than robbing the story of its meaning, have only enhanced it. Somebody has called it the greatest recognition scene in all literature.

A Meeting in Crisis

Jesus, on this first Easter morning, found Mary Magdalene in pain. A crisis was upon her. She was lonely and weeping in a garden. Jesus, who had loved her and given her new life, had just three days earlier been put to death without justice and mercy. Her world had fallen apart.

It is interesting to follow Jesus on the day of His resurrection. He went from crisis to crisis. On that night He found His disciples hiding behind locked doors. They had retreated from life and were afraid to venture forth. Their hope lay in broken bits in their hearts. They who had been so strong were now so weak. They who had been so hopeful were now so despairing.

Luke tells about two disciples going to Emmaus that day. Jesus joined them on their lonely way, and they were so caught up in their grief that they did not recognize who was with them.

But this was typical of Jesus. He was always finding people in dire straits who were far out on the extremities, not being able to manage their situations. He was continually with people in crisis.

Typical of Jesus' care, He went to His disciples who were about to lose their lives in a storm at sea. He stood on the shore for a while and observed them rowing against the waves and wind. They seemed to be no match for the storm. Their boat was about to capsize. All seemed to be lost. Then Jesus came toward them walking on the waves. They were afraid of Him, believing Him to be a ghost. Through the howling wind they heard Him say: "Take heart, it is I; have no fear" (Mark 6:50).

Stories like this are in our Gospels for a purpose. God knows that we face emotional and spiritual storms as real as those on that lake. Mark reminds us that Jesus cares, that He comes to us when the rowing is hard, that He is a stiller of the storms of life. He knew how to speak peace to that troubled sea and He knows how to speak to the troubled heart.

Brother Lawrence knew the peace that Christ can give to the heart amid the storms of life. "If the vessel of your soul is still tossed with the winds and storms," he wrote, "let us awake the Lord, who reposes in it, and he will quickly calm the storm."[1]

A prayer of Thomas à Kempis reflects the same truth:

Grant to me above all things that can be desired, to rest in thee, and in thee to have my heart at peace. Thou art the true peace of the heart; Thou its only rest; out of thee all things are hard and restless. In this peace, in this self-same thing, that is, in thee, the chiefest Eternal God, I will sleep and rest. Amen.

Meeting of Grace

Mark tells us that Mary Magdalene was a woman out of whom Jesus had cast seven devils.

Mary Magdalene has traditionally been pictured as a bad woman, as a harlot. She may have been, but we would not be dogmatic about that. The seven devils could mean that a moral and spiritual shadow lay over her life, or they could mean that she was a physically sick woman. Whether the shadow was moral, spiritual, or physical in nature, Mary was not a whole person. She was a woman in need, and she did not have the resources with which to heal herself. Whether physically or morally sick, Mary needed grace. And in meeting Jesus that morning, she was confronted by the Person of grace.

Paul tells us that we are saved by grace. In his clearest statement about this, he wrote: "For by grace you have been saved through faith; and this is not your own doing, it is the gift of God—not because of works, lest any man should boast" (Eph. 2:8).

Paul's great religious problem was: How will a sinful man stand justified before a just God? His first answer was to acquire virtues through good works that would at last favorably commend him to God. Paul worked hard at his salvation. He studied, prayed, obeyed the law devotedly, kept vigils, and buffeted his body. Yet peace of mind and heart eluded him. The very law he kept so diligently seemed to turn on him and enslave him. He was like a fish in a net. The harder he worked to free himself, the more entangled he became. Then he met the risen Lord along the Damascus road. And in that moment he knew all his virtues were like artificial pearls. They were of no avail. Paul found another way to God that day which was trust, not works. In trusting God's gracious actions in Christ, for the first time he experienced peace and salvation. It was not of his doing but of God's. It was of grace. Also, for the first time he knew he stood as a justified person before God and for no other reason than that he had believed in Christ. Out of that experience came two great doctrines of salvation by grace and justification by faith.

We all have to come to God the way Paul did. That is the way I came. I brought only empty hands to Him, and He said they were enough. His salvation could not be bought. It is of grace; it is a gift.

But if Mary Magdalene's seven devils caused a physical illness, grace was still relevant. If it did not heal her, it could enable her to accept her illness and bear it in dignity without resentment or bitterness.

Paul had an illness that he called a thorn in the flesh. His illness was probably bad eyesight, but we cannot be sure. Paul said he asked the Lord three times to heal him. While Christ did not heal him, He assured Paul that His grace was sufficient for him.

John Bunyan became very depressed after reading Hebrews, especially 6:4. He wondered if he were among the elect. He was tempted to commit suicide until he read 2 Corinthians 12:9. "My grace is sufficient for you, for my power is made perfect in weakness." Only those words were powerful enough to save Bunyan from the violence of his own hands.

A Personal Encounter

Jesus called Mary Magdalene by name. The calling of her name stirred great feelings in her, and apparently, Mary was making ready to rush toward Him and embrace Him. But He forbade her.

Jesus had first addressed her simply as "woman." "Woman, why are you weeping?" He asked. "Whom do you seek?" She was not moved by this. She thought Jesus was the gardener. It was only as Jesus called her by name that she became fully aware of who she was and who He was.

The address of *woman* was too abstract and impersonal. Mary was, of course, a woman, but she was a special woman with a name. It was her name more than anything else that identified her. We may say, "I know that face," or "I am familiar with that voice," or "I recognize that footfall," but it is the name that identifies us best.

This leads us to self-identification which can be one of the most serious problems in life. Who am I? That is an important question. At first, the answer may seem reasonably easy. I am a man, I am a husband, I am a father, I am an American citizen, and I am a minister. Yet, I cannot stop there. I begin to sense the mystery of my own life, thoughts that are deep and elusive, behavior I cannot understand, and longing for the unseen and eternal. When I begin to understand myself, two things become obvious: my life is bound up with others, and I belong to God. I learn who I am in terms of relationships.

Not only do I want people to know my name, I want God to know it. Here is one of the deepest longings of the human heart. We want to believe that God is personal and that He knows us personally. The Bible bears powerful testimony to the fact that God is personal, that He is more than first cause, a principle, an impersonal force, or cosmic energy. Jesus said God is like a father who is concerned, who loves us, and who knows our name. Jesus believed that if God observed the falling bird with a broken wing, He certainly knows and cares about us. We are worth more than many sparrows.

Remember Moses on the backside of a desert before a burning bush that was not consumed? He became aware of a presence that was addressing him: "Moses! Moses!" (Ex. 3:4). It was God.

This personal encounter with God runs throughout the Bible. Jeremiah said that God reached forth His hand and touched his mouth. Isaiah said the grace of God was near enough to touch his life and cleanse him. Paul, with his face in the dust along a wayside, heard the risen Lord asking: "Saul, Saul, why do you persecute me?" (Acts 9:4).

I remember John Campbell. He was one of the warmest, most human people I have known. I remember one Sunday morning, while he was a high-school student, he walked down the aisle of our church and told me he was accepting Jesus Christ as Savior and Lord of his life. He wanted to be baptized into the life of our church.

John went away to college and studied law. For a good many years he was employed by a bank in Richmond, Virginia. Then in the midst of his best years, death struck him down. He was only in his middle fifties. They brought him back home for his funeral and burial. When I drove up on the premises of the funeral home, I saw a chartered bus parked in front. I wondered why it was there. I learned that many of John's fellow employees at the bank had chartered the bus and traveled almost halfway across the state to attend his funeral.

A sister of his later related a story to me about the morning John had made his profession of faith. I had never heard it before. He told her that as I preached that morning it was as if God were paging him, calling him by name, and saying, "John, I have good news for you."

Encounter With a Woman

As I have earlier said, we are surprised. We would have expected Jesus to appear to a disciple. Mark tells us that He appeared first of all to Mary Magdalene. He instructed her to tell the good news to others, and other women were involved. Women became the first preachers of the good news of Easter. John tells us that Mary Magdalene went and said to the disciples, "I have seen the Lord" (John 20:18).

Sherman E. Johnson says of Mary Magdalene: "She is an important figure in the gospel accounts because the story of the empty tomb is traced back to her."

I teach in a theological school, and I have some young women in my classes. They are as highly motivated and as dedicated as the men. They have a strong sense of God's calling to the gospel ministry. Like Mary Magdalene, they are following Jesus' instruction to share the good news.

Mary Magdalene was out early on Easter morning. In grief and sorrow she went to minister to the body of the Lord. She found instead the risen Lord. Her grief became joy. Her uncertainty became a clear message to the others, "I have seen the Lord."

Note

1. Brother Lawrence, *The Practice of the Presence of God* (Old Tappan, NJ: Fleming H. Revell Co., 1958), 45.

14
Resurrection Now!

(Rom. 6:1-4)

Christianity often uses three tenses—past, present, and future—to speak of its great realities. Salvation is best expressed in three tenses: We have been saved, we are being saved, and we shall be saved. The Kingdom falls within this framework: it has come, is coming, and will come.

Jesus Christ does not escape these three dimensions of time: "Jesus Christ is the same yesterday and today and for ever" (Heb. 13:8). Even God speaks of himself in three tenses: "I am the Alpha and the Omega, says the Lord God, who is and who was and who is to come, the Almighty" (Rev. 1:8).

It helps us to understand resurrection in the same way. Resurrection has occurred, is occurring, and will occur.

In this sermon we shall think of resurrection in the present tense. We are now being lifted from death into new life. There is such a thing as moral and spiritual resurrection. It can happen now.

It will help us to remember a simple fact: resurrection has to do with new life.

New Life

New life is possible because God makes new things possible. Our sermon falls within one of the broadest and most sweeping themes of the Bible.

Isaiah pictures God as creating new things, "Behold, I am doing a new thing;" He declares. "Now it springs forth, do you not perceive it?" (43:19).

Ezekiel heard God saying: "I will sprinkle clean water upon you, and you shall be clean from all your uncleannesses, and from all your idols I will cleanse you. A new heart I will give you, . . . and I will take out of your flesh the heart of stone and give you a heart of flesh" (Ezek. 36:25-26).

Jesus talked about giving new life. (He called it eternal life.) And Paul said if a person is in Christ he or she is a new creation.

The theme of the new continues throughout the Bible. In the twenty-first chapter of Revelation, you hear a powerful voice announcing: "Behold, I make all things new" (v. 5). Imagine it! Everything is sparkling new—no longer the old, the castaway, or the obsolescent.

New Life Now

New life has been given now, resurrection can happen now. The New Testament uses three striking metaphors to tell of this radically new reality: new birth, new creation, and resurrection.

Jesus talked with Nicodemus, a distinguished jurist, who belonged to a court that would be equivalent to the Supreme Court of the United States. He was the finest flowering of his culture and religion. Nicodemus was no doubt an old man, and Jesus shocked him when He said, "You must be born again." The new life would be born of the Spirit, and it would be mysterious like the wind. "The wind blows where it wills," He said, "and you hear the sound of it, but you do not know whence it comes or whither it goes; so it is with every one who is born of the Spirit" (John 3:8).

Paul speaks of new creation: "If any one is in Christ, he is a new creation; the old has passed away, behold, the new has come" (2 Cor. 5:17). Paul was being autobiographical. He knew about what he was speaking; it had happened to him. When Paul met the risen Lord along the Damascus road, Christ turned him around in his tracks, causing him to pivot on a 180-degree angle, set him in a new direction, and gave him a new heart. He was indeed a new man. It was more than moral veneer, more than reformation, and more than face-lifting. It was new creation, transformation, and resurrection.

The third metaphor the New Testament uses is resurrection. It was the basic meaning of Christian baptism. Baptism dramatized the death, burial, and resurrection of Jesus Christ. It proclaimed the heart of the Christian gospel. And it told of something significant that had happened to the believer: he or she was burying an old life and being resurrected to a new life. "We were buried therefore with him by baptism into death," Paul declares, "so that as Christ was raised from the dead by the glory of the Father, we too might walk in newness of life" (Rom. 6:4). This was not something in the past, nor something in the future, it was a present reality. It was resurrection now. It was so radically new that Paul could speak of it as resurrection.

Paul on another occasion put the same truth in this way: "Once you were darkness, but now you are light in the Lord" (Eph. 5:8).

John states it this way: "We know that we have passed out of death into life, because we love the brethren (1 John 3:14).

Peter remembered: "Once you were no people but now you are God's people; once you had not received mercy but now you have received mercy" (1 Pet. 2:10).

For Paul as well as others there was a then and a now, and the now was so much more wonderful than the then. "You, who once were estranged and hostile in mind," Paul writes, "doing evil deeds, he has now reconciled in his body of flesh by his death, in order to present you holy and blameless and irreproachable before him" (Col. 1:21-22). There was a before and after, and the after was so much more exciting than the before. Before there had been death, but after Christ and His resurrection there was life. It was life so radically new and different that it could be spoken of as resurrected life.

The new life was like the beginning of a new day. You see streaks of light in the east, the flush of the dawn. It is not the full dawn nor the glory of the full day. When the glory of the full day has come, the mist will be lifted and the shadows will be driven away, and the earth will be bathed in warmth and light. But the light that had been seen in the flush of morning is not different from the light that will make possible the full day. It is the same light, there is just more of it when the day has fully come.

Only heaven will reveal the full glory of the resurrected life. There we shall see God face-to-face and offer Him perfect praise. And we shall love our fellows with perfect love and serve them with perfect service. But that life, as perfect and wonderful as it will be, begins here. We see now and are experiencing now the first light, the pre-dawn of that perfect day.

Marks of the Resurrected Life

The resurrected life can be identified; it has certain marks that characterize it.

First of all, there is a new life-style.

Paul speaks of the new life-style in radical terms. Some had been children of darkness but now they were children of light. They had been slaves of the powers of evil but Christ had set them free.

There is a fragment of an early hymn that goes like this:

> Awake, O sleeper, and arise from the dead,
> and Christ shall give you light (Eph. 5:14).

Peter speaks of God "who called you out of darkness into his marvelous light" (1 Pet. 2:9).

As children of light they were to live differently, they were to develop a life-style befitting their new status.

Paul talks of how they were to give up drunkenness, revelry, immorality, slandering, and maliciousness. They were to be through with anger, hostility, bitterness, and they were to live in peace with one another. They were not to steal or take that which did not belong to them. They were to do honest work and give to the needy.

Yet, as important as these were, they were not the chief marks of the resurrected life. The chief quality was love, the kind of love the world had seen in Jesus. It was the kind of love that loved not only the good, beautiful, and healthy but the bad, marred, and the sick. It loved those whom the world did not love, those who did not love themselves. It was an adventuresome, courageous, and self-giving love. The New Testament calls it *agape* love. They were to live by the new commandment Jesus had given: "A new commandment I give to you, that you love one another; even as I have loved you, that you also love one another" (John 13:34).

Paul sets forth this way of love best in the thirteenth chapter of First Corinthians. (I have always thought that Paul pictured Jesus in his mind's eye as he wrote this wonderful poem on love. It is a perfect description of Jesus.) "Love is patient and kind; love is not jealous or boastful; it is not arrogant or rude. Love does not insist on its own way; it is not irritable or resentful; it does not rejoice at wrong, but rejoices in the right. Love bears all things, believes all things, hopes all things, endures all things" (13:4-7).

John could say: "Beloved, let us love one another; for love is of God, and he who loves is born of God and knows God. He who does not love does not know God; for God is love." (1 John 4:7-8).

Love is the greatest ethical quality of the resurrected life.

Second, the resurrected life is empowered by the Spirit.

Where does the power come from for the living of this ethical life? From human strength? No, that would be absolutely impossible. It comes from the Holy Spirit Who is God's gift to His people.

The gift of the Spirit came at Pentecost, and He came in power, like a mighty rushing wind from heaven. Therefore the Spirit gives us the power to achieve that which we could not, even in our best and most heroic efforts.

Those who have been given the resurrected life are urged to walk in the Spirit, live in the Spirit, and be led by the Spirit. Paul urged the early Christians to set their minds on the Spirit which is "life and peace" (Rom. 8:6). "For all who are led by the Spirit of God," Paul says, "are sons of God" (Rom. 8:14).

While Christians are to take themselves in hand, undergo discipline, and strive to imitate Christ, their real success comes not from their own efforts. It comes from the power of the Spirit. Therefore, the New Testament speaks of the new ethical life of love as the fruit of the Spirit: "The fruit of the Spirit is love, joy, peace, patience, kindness, goodness, faithfulness, gentleness, self-control" (Gal. 5:22). It is an impressive list of virtues, and it is significant that love heads the list.

As already suggested, we do not come upon the ethical ideal by shoving, pushing, and striving. A time comes when we hear a voice speaking to us: "You are trying too hard. Relax. Take it easy. Let the Spirit work in and through you."

The coming of the Spirit is like the incoming tide that lifts the stranded barge. It is like the wind that blows the boat that has not sailed despite the fact that its sails have been unfurled against the sky.

We keep coming back to Jesus' new commandment. It seems so impossible. A person says: "I often find it hard to give common, everyday love. I frequently do not love my wife and child the way I should. I do not care for my neighbor down the street the way I ought. Sometimes I wonder if I can love at all, I am so filled with bitterness and hatred. Please don't tell me to love the way Jesus did."

We identify with that person. We understand what he means. We have been where he is.

Yesterday was a bad day. I was almost burned up by bitterness and resentment. I knew how irrational it was, and some day that hatred, like a volcano, could erupt and destroy me. Before going to bed, I said to myself: "This has been a terrible day. I have hated all day long, but tomorrow will be different. Tomorrow I will love." After a fitful night, I awake early in the morning. What is the first thing in my mind? The same old hatred.

The Holy Spirit comes to my rescue. He enables me to do that which I cannot do myself. He makes the impossible possible. Paul knew this. "God's love," he wrote, "has been poured into our hearts through the Holy Spirit which has been given to us" (Rom. 5:5).

The image could well be that of a cup, filled with anger and bitterness. Then as the Holy Spirit begins pouring the love of God into my heart, the bitterness and anger are gradually displaced by the love of God. He continues to pour until the emotional dregs are completely gone, and my heart is brimming over with love. On that day the Holy Spirit enables me to say to a person with whom I have been at odds for a long time: "Your face looks different today. I really do love and care for you."

Third, the resurrected life is lived in Christ.

The resurrected life is an ethical life of love; it is a life empowered by the Spirit; and it is a life lived in Christ.

When Paul spoke of his relationship with Christ, his favorite expression was "in Christ." Paul uses that term or its equivalent 164 times. One of the finest books ever written on Paul is *A Man in Christ* by James Stewart.

What did Paul mean by that phrase? Possibly at least two things. First, it meant a personal, intimate, mystical relationship with Christ. Second, it meant belonging to the church which is the body of Christ. To be in Christ's body was to be in Him.

Paul knew a mystical presence in the resurrected Lord. Paul was aware that the living Christ was always with him. As he tramped between the cities of Asia Minor and along their streets, he knew there walked beside him the unseen risen Lord. When he touched the shores of southeast Europe, he knew he was not alone. Christ went with him.

With this mystical relationship in mind, Paul wrote: "I have been crucified with Christ; it is no longer I who live, but Christ who lives in me; and the life I now live in the flesh I live by faith in the Son of God, who loved me and gave himself for me" (Gal. 2:20). It was as if Christ was in Paul, and Paul was in Christ.

Being in Christ could have a less mystical meaning. It could mean belonging to the church which is the body of Christ.

The body of Christ was Paul's favorite expression for the church. What does it mean? It is a very difficult and elusive term. But its most obvious meaning is that Christ wants to live in the church the way we live in our bodies. He wants us to be His hands and feet, His eyes and ears, His voice and His heart. He wants to love our broken world through us. In some real sense, the incarnation is to continue in the church.

Paul gives his most elaborate statement of this concept in the twelfth chapter of First Corinthians. While the basic idea is incarnational, let me make three other observations: the church, while many, is one; all the members are needed, and each member is indispensable.

The early church came from everywhere. Many cultures, classes, and races were in it. Yet Paul, conscious of their diverse ways and backgrounds, would not let them forget that Christ had made them one. One of the severest tests of the modern church is whether or not it will transcend the barriers of our culture and be one in Christ. It does not do well here.

Further, all the members are needed. Each has an important task to perform. "As it is, . . . The eye cannot say to the hand, 'I have no need of you,' nor again the head to the feet, 'I have no need of you'" (1 Cor. 12:20-21). All need each other, and each is needed.

Finally, each member is more than important; he or she is indispensable. "The parts of the body which seem to be weak are indispensable" (v. 22). Here is indicated the wonderful value Christ puts on every life. Each is indispensable.

When the church is authentic, it takes the poorest, weakest, youngest, most illiterate, most nonproductive and says: "You are more than useful. You are indispensable. We couldn't be who we are without you." I recall the day that wonderful truth broke in upon my mind. I said, "If for no other reason than that I would want to belong to the church."

I remember doing a week of preaching in a church not far from where I live. It was a moderate-size church with substantial people making up its membership. The ex-mayor was a member, as were some professional and business people. These I have forgotten. The one person I remember best of all was a retarded man in his forties who stood at one of the doors handing out church bulletins. You couldn't get through that door without shaking hands with him. He was indispensable for the life of that church. The church couldn't be what it is without him. If he should move away, a part of the church would move with him. And when that poor man dies, a part of that church will die with him.

We are seeking ways to revitalize the church. In our time I can't think of a better way than to go back upstream to the springs of our faith, and to stand there where the water is clear, and to remember those wonderful images the New Testament uses for the church. Then take those images and recast them for our time.

One of the most powerful images is the church as the body of Christ. One wonders if the modern church can ever be revitalized in our time unless it is willing to be the incarnation of Christ in our world.

15
The Resurrected Lord Along Our Dusty Ways

(Luke 24:13-43)

On Easter, Jesus overtook two of His disciples going to Emmaus, a small town seven miles west of Jerusalem. They were so caught up in their grief and sorrow that they were not aware of His presence. Jesus spoke to them, but they made no immediate response. "They stood still, looking sad" (v. 17).

Jesus asked them what they were talking about. They were surprised. How could anyone have been in Jerusalem for the last few days and not know what everyone was talking about. So one of His disciples, Cleopas, asked: "Are you the only visitor to Jerusalem who does not know the things that have happened there in these days?" (v. 18). A prophet, Jesus of Nazareth, who had caught the imagination of the nation, had been put to death with two criminals just north of the city along one of the main highways. The place was so cosmopolitan that they wrote His accusation in three languages: Hebrew, Latin, and Greek.

Jesus talked of how the Scriptures were being fulfilled in His death and resurrection. It was He to whom the great drama of Scripture had been moving.

Time passed fast as they engaged in such exciting conversation. Sundown found them at the entrance of the village. It seemed obvious that Jesus was going on, but at their insistence He went in to have supper with them. They asked Him to say grace, and as He did they recognized Him. There was something so familiar in the way He broke the bread, blessed it, and passed it. And with the recognition, He vanished out of their sight.

All Easter stories are beautiful, but the Emmaus story by Luke is one of the most beautiful of them all. MacLean Gilmour speaks of it as "a story of singular grace and charm."[1]

With Men of Sorrow

Easter morning had broken upon a turbulent scene. Emotions ran a wide gamut. There was joy and sadness, hope and despair, faith and doubt.

The two men whom Jesus joined along the Emmaus road were caught in one of the paralyzing emotions of that first Easter. They were exceedingly sad and sorrowful, being blinded by their sadness. "But their eyes were kept from recognizing him" (v. 16). Their senses were dulled to His presence. Their despair seemed too deep for hope.

They had built a new world around Jesus, and now with His death their world had caved in about them. Their dreams lay in broken bits at their feet.

For what had they hoped? Hear them: "But we had hoped that he was the one to redeem Israel" (v. 21). Redemption meant freedom. They had been looking for a messiah who would deliver them from the Roman yoke. They were a conquered and enslaved people. Wherever they went, they saw Roman soldiers ready to suppress any kind of revolt. They heard the cadence of the soldiers marching on the cobblestones of their city streets. These soldiers were billeted in their villages and towns. Then there were the hated tax collectors, appointed by Roman officials, who administered an oppressive tax system that drained away so much of their wealth into the coffers of Rome. A restlessness and turbulence lay just beneath the surface of Jewish national life. The slightest thing could have lighted a conflagration. They had hoped Jesus would release the pent-up fear, anger, and hostility of the people, organize an army, and drive the hated Romans beyond their borders. They, as did the rest of the disciples, looked for a political messiah who would liberate them from their captors. How they wanted to be free! Redemption meant political freedom more than anything else.

The idea of redemption was very appealing to Jesus. Indeed that was His main mission in the world. Yet, He envisioned redemption in larger terms than political freedom. He came to set men and women free from moral and spiritual servitude. He knew there were moral powers as real as handcuffs and chains that shackled and enslaved men and women. His ultimate hope was to free them from the two most enslaving powers: sin and death. This He would do through His death and resurrection. Once this had been accomplished, Jesus knew that a hope would be lighted in the human heart that nothing could ever put out. We should not forget that Easter brings freedom from death.

Jesus and Scripture

Jesus turned to Scripture to interpret the strange happening in Jerusalem during the last few days. "O foolish men, and slow of heart to believe all that the prophets have spoken!" He said. "Was it not necessary that the Christ should suffer these things and enter into his glory?" (v. 25). Then Luke made the telling comment, "And beginning with Moses and all the prophets, he interpreted to them in all the scriptures the things concerning himself" (v. 27). The scriptures were essentially pointing to Him, being fulfilled in Him.

Luke spoke of "all the scriptures." What did he mean? He tells us. He means the Law of Moses and the Prophets. They were the official Scriptures in Jesus' time. The Law of Moses became Scripture by 400 B.C., while the prophets became Scripture around 200 B.C. A third division of Scripture, to be known as the Writings, was emerging. It consisted of poetry, wisdom, drama, prophecy, history, and stories. Some sixty years later they would become an official part of Scripture at the Council of Jamina, A.D. 90.

In what sense does Jesus fulfill Scripture? We must remember that the Old Testament is about salvation history. Its themes of salvation and redemption are fulfilled in Jesus. He came as the Savior, as the Redeemer, to set us free. One of the loveliest doxologies in all of literature sings about this: "To him who loves us and has freed us from our sins by his blood and made us a kingdom, priests to his God and Father, to him be glory and dominion for ever and ever. Amen" (Rev. 1:5-6).

The important thing to remember, as already stated, is that the

Scriptures were pointing to Jesus and were being fulfilled in Him. The basic purpose of Scripture is to bear witness to Jesus.

This leads us to a very crucial observation: we so often do not understand our Scriptures in that way. The Scriptures become an end in themselves. They witness to themselves. The Bible becomes an idol. We worship it. This kind of idolatry is known as bibliolatry.

Jesus said one day to some very devout people: "You search the scriptures, because you think that in them you have eternal life; and it is they that bear witness to me; yet you refuse to come to me that you may have life" (John 5:39-40).

They believed that the sacred writings offered them life, but that was beyond the power of a book to give. Life was in Him alone. Yet the Book had an indispensable role—to bear witness to Him. That is what He told those two disciples along the Emmaus road. And that is what He is still telling us.

Jesus never wrote but once so far as we know, and that was in the sand. A careless foot or a passing shower soon erased it forever. What did He write? We can never know. Jesus was probably wise in trusting His truth to the precarious memories of His followers rather than to a manuscript bearing His name. What if He had left a monograph? Human nature being what it is we would have made a fetish out of it and worshiped it.

Recognized at a Table

Who the stranger was remained a complete mystery until the Emmaus travelers asked Him to say grace. The grace was probably one they had heard all their lives: "Praised be Thou, O Lord, our God, King of the universe, who brings forth bread and food from the ground." There was something different in the way He said it. They recognized Him, and He vanished out of their sight.

The table was as important in that day as it is today. At the table they remembered they were not disembodied spirits. They had bodies that became tired, grew hungry, and needed food. The reality of hunger and bread bound them with humanity everywhere.

Not only are physical needs met at the table but social ones as well. It is so much better when we eat together than when we eat alone. When we sit at a common table, whether with friends or strangers, our relationships are changed. We are never the same again.

The origins of terms are interesting. Sometimes they will uncover basic and pertinent meanings long forgotten. For example, the term *companion* comes from *companis* which means with bread. One of the best places for friendship and companionship is the dinner table.

The dinner table for Jesus was a place of social acceptance and reconciliation. The fact that He ate with publicans and sinners spoke more effectively than anything He could have said. The dinner table was the place where the last barrier to social acceptance was broken down.

The dinner table was a place of religious significance. No matter how hard you had worked for the meal on the table, when you traced the bread to its ultimate source you came upon the open hands of God. The dinner table, therefore, was a place for prayer and thanksgiving.

It has always been a fact of great interest to me that when Jesus gave the church two ordinances, one of them was a meal: the Lord's Supper. The church down the centuries has variously interpreted that Supper, but all have agreed that Christ meets us there as nowhere else.

Burning Hearts

After the supper where Christ had blessed the bread and then vanished out of their sight, they began to say to each other, "Did not our hearts burn within us while he talked to us on the road, while he opened to us the scriptures?" (v. 32).

Burning hearts remind us of something that psalmist said: "My heart became hot within me. / As I mused, the fire burned; / then I spoke with my tongue" (Ps. 39:3). The words reflect the experience of Jeremiah: "There is in my heart as it were a burning fire / shut up in my bones, / and I am weary with holding it in, / and I cannot" (Jer. 20:9).

There should be a total response to God's Word. The mind should say: "It is credible. I believe it." The heart should say: "I feel its truth and exult in it." The will should say: "I will clothe it in flesh and blood. I will live it."

Of the three responses, that of the heart is the most important. The mind, untouched by the heart, can be as cold as a winter's night. Only a burning heart can melt the iciness of the mind. And only a burning heart can move a sluggish and cowardly will.

As a boy I saw preachers emotionally manipulate people. Deathbed stories were often resorted to, causing fear and sadness. I reacted negatively to that kind of preaching. So when I finished the seminary I resolved that my sermons would be carefully prepared and logically presented. I would appeal to the minds of the people, not their feelings. I was right in not wanting to manipulate people emotionally, but I had a very inadequate concept of motivation. I had forgotten a very salient fact about life: the heart is the dynamic center of personality, and people are not moved unless the heart has been touched. People still need to respond to the gospel with burning hearts.

Along Our Dusty Ways

I remember how shocked I was a few years ago when I realized that in the Bible God revealed Himself, not so much at altars and holy places, as in the secular places along common ways.

In our Scripture, Jesus appeared to two of His followers, not at some holy place but along a dusty country road. Later in the day He was recognized at something as commonplace as a dinner table. These encounters were far away from the altar of a temple.

You recall Jacob's meeting God in a wilderness. It was a most unlikely place to find God or be found by Him. Jacob slept beneath the stars on the hard, rocky ground, with a stone for his pillow. There was no sacred Scripture, no chanting priest, no altar with burning incense, and no choir singing a hallelujah chorus. Yet the next morning Jacob exclaimed: "How awesome is this place! This is none other than the house of God, and this is the gate of heaven" (Gen. 28:17).

The Exodus, the towering event of the Old Testament, could not have occurred at a more secular place than the Red Sea, skirted by caravan routes with commercial barges sailing on its waters. On that day of deliverance one heard the grinding of chariot wheels, the profanity of cavalry officers, and the groaning of oppressed people on their way to freedom.

God took Amos as he followed his sheep and dressed sycamore trees. Amos declared he was not a prophet, nor a prophet's son. Yet God found him in that rustic place and said, "Go, prophesy to my people Israel" (Amos 7:15).

Jesus was born not in the precinct of a temple but in a manger, was not dressed in holy garments but wrapped in swaddling clothes. He was more a layperson than a rabbi. He spoke the language of the people. He was put to death not between two candles on an altar but between two criminals on a hill that was named for a skull. He was not buried in a temple crypt but in a borrowed tomb in a garden. He ascended to His Father not from the pinnacle of the Temple but from the Mount of Olives.

Paul met the living Christ along a road to Damascus. And while prostrate—not before an altar but on the ground with his face in the dust—Paul acknowledged Christ as Lord!

Yet, this is not to deny the value of sacred places and holy hours. They are very important. It was in the temple that Isaiah heard seraphim crying one to the other: "Holy, holy, holy is the Lord of hosts; / the whole earth is full of his glory" (Isa. 6:3). It was in that Temple that Isaiah experienced forgiveness, heard God calling, and was commissioned to be God's messenger. And when Jesus got ready to give His inaugural address, He went back to Nazareth and delivered it in the synagogue where He had been brought up.

It is not, therefore, important where God meets us but that we are encountered by Him, not where we are forgiven but that our lives are touched by His grace, not where we are commissioned but that God sends us into the world with a message of hope. We should live our lives in expectancy not knowing where our risen Lord will join us.

Note

1. S. MacLean Gilmour, *The Interpreter's Bible*, vol. 8 (Nashville: Abingdon Press, 1952), 421.